Me and My Addiction

Published in 2023 by Welford Publishing

ISBN: Paperback 978-1-7390970-7-3

Editor: Christine McPherson

A catalogue for this book is available from the British Library.

Me and My Addiction

To Kate

Thanks for all your Support

Stewart Lee

Disclaimer

This book is designed to provide helpful information on the subjects discussed. It is general reference information which should not be used to diagnose any medical problem and is not intended as a substitute for consulting with a medical or professional practitioner.

Some names and identifying details have been changed to protect the privacy of the individuals.

For Rosie. You put up with me working away for so many nights in a row and allowed me the time to start writing this book. And I can't thank you enough for all the support you've given me during this journey of getting the book published. I wouldn't have got through the last few months without you. I love you to infinity and beyond.

For Anna. Your belief in me helped me take the first step on my recovery journey. Sadly, you passed away before being able to see me succeed. I hope I have made you proud.

For Mum. The faith you always had in me becoming a better man will always inspire me to keep pushing on and strive to keep improving my life. Miss you, Mum.

For my children, Owen, Charlie, and Isabelle. You three are my reason for everything I do. I hope I'm not too embarrassing.

Contents

What's the point? 15

01. It should have terrified me..........................21
02. The disease of addiction 29
03. Addiction is environmental? 37
04. Always a step too far 44
05. A progressive illness................................53
06. The alcoholic pub manager 61
07. No consequence is big enough 70
08. Moving the goalposts................................78
09. They wanted me go to rehab, and I said... 87
10. Into recovery.......................................96
11. This beast keeps growing inside of us 105
12. My last rodeo 114
13. Resentment hurts me the most 122
14. What's the point? 129

What's the point?

My heart was pounding like it was about to burst out of my chest as I drove up the long driveway. Trees overhead and on either side, you couldn't really see anything too far ahead; the large building slowly coming into view. I hadn't seen this building for around 14 years, and as I got closer and could see all the windows, I tried to recall which one used to be my bedroom. But I couldn't even remember the layout of the place, so I couldn't work it out.

One thing that I can still remember even now is the feeling I had when I first set eyes on this place. Back then, I was a different person, full of fear of the unknown. I knew what I wanted to do, but had no idea how to do it.

The feeling I had this time was exactly the same, but fear for a completely different reason. On this occasion I was back at the recovery treatment centre to speak to the current residents and share my story about how bad my life had become, my time in the centre, and what I'd done since. I wanted to show them that I had once been exactly where they were, yet I'd managed to turn my life around and was no longer a slave to addiction.

On arrival, I was taken into an office with a few members of staff, and we shared a pleasant and informal chat about what I'd done since I left there 14 years before. I felt comfortable at that stage because there were only four of us in the room. But at one point I thought I was going to run out of things to say and I panicked. How on earth was I going to cope speaking to a room full of people?

We left the office and went through into the lounge, where a staff member had gathered all the residents who wanted to hear me speak. Looking around quickly, I picked what looked like a nice comfy chair. But I soon realised that I had picked the only seat that was in direct sunlight which was beaming in through the massive window to my left. Feeling too self-conscious to move, I was sweating with nerves and the heat before I even started to speak.

One of the staff members told me later that it was normally a struggle to keep their attention for any longer than about half an hour, but somehow I'd managed to keep them silenced for two hours, hanging off every word I said. Most were young males, with two young females, and we were joined by a few other staff members I hadn't seen in the office.

I began by talking about my life before I found the treatment centre, and then explained what I'd done since. After I finished my story, the session ended with a sort of question time, and one of the residents asked me if I had ever considered writing a book about my life. I told him that I had thought about it a few times, but had avoided it because I was afraid it would just become an ego-driven exercise.

A few years before, I had been at a recovery meeting one night when a new member arrived to speak to us. The guy was smart, funny, knew so much about himself, and he had a really good level of recovery. Everyone in the room was blown away by what he had to say. After the meeting, he and I exchanged phone numbers and we met up a few times to discuss recovery. On one occasion, he invited me to his home, so I drove out there and met his wife and child. He had this massive house in the country, with a garage bigger than my whole flat, and loads of land all around. If I had to guess, I would say it had to be worth over a million quid.

He told me how he had started a successful business and now paid people to run it while he could sit back and enjoy living there. He was a real success story in recovery. Then we went into his office, and he showed me his vision board with all the things he wanted to achieve. And I saw that writing and publishing a book was on his to-do list.

A few months later, his book was released, so I bought a copy as soon as I could. I wanted to support him as well as to read his story in full. It was a well written book, and it was an inspirational story of how someone had turned their life around. Not long after the book came out, though, I didn't really see him at meetings any more, and he became much harder to get hold of. After thinking about the book a bit more, I realised that it was all about *him* – about what he had done, how low he'd got, how he had turned it around, and how he had become wealthy.

What made it even worse was that a month or so after the book launch, I was going through a situation that I knew he had also experienced early in his recovery. So I sent him a message to ask if it was possible we could have a chat at some point, because I believed he could relate to what I was going through. He read the message and never responded.

A few months later, I received a message from him to say he was holding a men's retreat on his property and asked if I would like to book a place. Clearly, he could contact me when he was trying to sell me something, but not when I needed a chat. The more I thought about it, it started to feel like he'd turned up at our meetings all those months before just to be a salesman for his book and his retreats. That is not what recovery is for me.

Once you have recovery, the only way to keep it is to give it away and help the next person who is struggling. If someone asks for help, I will tell them about my life and how low I got, how I felt, how I thought. But that isn't telling them so that I can brag and point to how well I've done. I do it so that the person can relate to what I'm saying and hopefully identify themselves as an addict… if that is what they believe they are.

It is not my job to tell people they are an addict or an alcoholic. The only way to do this is to tell them my story. But my story must be told without any ego.

And that is what I aim to do with this book. I simply want to explain the thoughts and feelings I experienced in the hope that it can help you, the reader. If you're someone that thinks they have a problem with alcohol, then I hope it can inspire you to make a change. If you are a family member of someone you think might need help, I hope it helps to give you a better understanding of the illness so that you can help and support your loved ones better.

I have become a firm believer that nothing happens in our lives by chance. The things that occur and the people we meet always happen for a reason. It isn't always evident what the reason is, but it does become clear at some point.

Not long after I'd been to the treatment centre to give my talk, the thought of writing a book was again rattling around my head. I was due to go on a dance weekender, where they also organised some workshops that needed to be booked in advance as a couple. I was going alone, so I posted on the organiser's social media page that I wanted to do some of the workshops but needed a female to volunteer to be my dance partner. I got a message from a lady named Cassandra, and we arranged which workshops we were going to do, and I got them booked.

We didn't meet for the first time until right before the first lesson, but we both really enjoyed the workshops. It turned out that some years ago Cassandra had been just like me, dreaming of writing a book but unsure how to start, and wondering if anyone would want to read what she had to say. Fast forward a few years, she is now an Author Coach, helping many other aspiring authors realise their dream and teaching them how to write their story. There is no way I can think that me meeting her was an accident!

After the dance weekend, I purchased her book, *Share Your World: How to write a life-changing book in 60 days*. In it, she explains that she had once read a book in which a celebrity was writing about something Cassandra was going through at the time. But she found it hard to relate to the author, because it is a completely different situation for someone who is rich and famous. They don't face a lot of the other everyday struggles that we normal people go through.

I've read books written by celebrities about how they have battled addiction and found recovery, and I agree it's hard to relate with them. It's the same illness, but when you have to build yourself up from nothing, it's a completely different story. They don't understand what it's like to be homeless and not know where their next meal is coming from. It's much easier for them sitting in their big house with all of life's luxuries on tap.

Cassandra's book inspired me even further to write my own story. When I was still in active addiction, I wish there had been a book available to me that was written by someone I could relate to. Alcoholism and addiction are the loneliest illnesses a person can suffer, and I truly believed for years that I was on my own facing this and that nobody else was the same as me. It was only once I realised that there were millions of others who thought, felt, and acted just like me, that I began to have some hope that change was possible. I came to believe that if there were lots of people feeling the same, then it really wasn't because we were nasty people who want to cause harm. It's because there is something fundamentally different about our nature. We are built differently to the normal person – if there is such a thing as normal.

My aim in this book is to give you a real-life account of addiction from a person who has been there and experienced it. I truly believe that what I have to say can help people, so I've finally realised that I have a story to tell that others need to hear. And hopefully it can do some good.

It doesn't matter what stage you, or your loved one, are at in your journey. Just have these three things in mind while you read my story: honesty, open-mindedness, and willingness. With this in mind, look for the similarities and not the differences, and you can take the next steps.

Let's do it together.

Stewart

Chapter 1

It should have terrified me

My memory of my life has become hazy over the years, especially when I'm trying to think back to incidents or times more than a few years ago. I'm not sure if this is due to me wanting to forget a lot of what happened, or that the amount of chemicals I put into my body has damaged my brain. Either way, I'll try and be as accurate as I can.

When I was around 17 years old, I was working full-time at a market stall selling fruit and vegetables. Don't imagine it like it was like you see on TV, with a cheeky chappie shouting out to the crowds to come and get their apples and pears, though. I didn't have any confidence at all, so I was a very quiet, shy boy at that time. The truth is I'd already been kicked out of college for either turning up drunk or not turning up at all. I'd only really started the course because my dad had banged on for years about how I needed to learn a trade, and I somehow managed to get an apprenticeship as an electrician. But I made a real mess of it. My dad worked in his trade as a pipe fitter/welder right up until he retired recently. I'm sure that's just his fancy way of saying he's a plumber, but I'll just ride with it for now.

I'd been working part-time at the market stall for a few years while I was at school, so it was easy to get more hours there. By that time I'd already lost any sort of ambition to achieve anything, apart from to get as drunk as I could and as often as I could. My only aim at that point was to work and earn beer tokens. If I'm honest…

Oops. Quick disclaimer at this point already. There might be a lot of people or places mentioned within this book that I still need to make amends to. If I disclose something bad that I've done in my life, please rest assured that you are on my amends list, and when I find the right time, you'll be hearing from me.

Where was I? Ah yes, being honest. I'd been working at the market long enough to know it was easy to steal money there. It's unlikely I was the only one on the fiddle, but I hold my hands up, I was a thieving little shit and had my hands in the till most days I was working. I always justified this in my head because I needed to fund my drinking habit, which I didn't at that stage realise was an addiction.

Seventeen years old, with no ambition, and dishonest to the core; already things weren't looking great for me. My only real desire at the time was to get into the local nightclub, even though I was still legally too young to drink alcohol. That was the culture back then, though, and most people my age worked all week and looked forward to the weekend when they could let their hair down and hit the town. The nightlife back then was buzzing, and the town was always packed with youngsters all getting smashed. I know it probably sounds normal – most 17-year-olds try to get into nightclubs – but I literally *lived* for it. It was all I wanted. My sister, who is two years older than me, was going to the club regularly, so that was another reason I was so keen. Another sign of a negative characteristic popping out: good old envy.

At that time, there was a dress code at all the nightclubs, and men had to wear collared shirts, trousers, and shoes. No jeans or trainers were allowed, so I would go out on a Saturday afternoon with my hard-earned/stolen money and purchase new shirts to get myself looking dapper for a night on the town. We would finish work around 6pm and then all go home to change and meet up in town not too long after. Thinking back to this weekly routine, what stands out to me is the sheer excitement I would feel all the way home. I couldn't get ready quickly enough. Most weekends I wouldn't even bother eating dinner! I just wanted to get home, change as quickly as possible, and get back out to town to start drinking.

I'd throw on my smart clobber and whatever the popular cheap aftershave was at the time, arm myself with my fake ID, and hit the town. Most weekends there was disappointment at not getting into some of the busier pubs, but we always had a route of the ones where we knew we could get served in. And the route would always lead to the quay, where the two most popular nightclubs were located.

When it came to making my attempt at getting into the club, week after week it was disappointment, and I'd be turned away for having really poor-quality fake ID. I looked quite young for my age, which didn't help. I couldn't get into an age 15 rated film at the cinema when I was younger, and I got asked for ID to buy cigarettes when I was too young to smoke. So querying my age was nothing new. But getting into that club was all I really wanted.

Then one weekend, it finally happened, and I got past the bouncers. As I went to the desk to pay for entry, I kept thinking that at some point a doorman was going to grab me by the collar of my shirt and throw me back out. Then I went to the cloakroom to put my really shit-looking leather jacket in for safekeeping. It was a bit embarrassing, though. I wanted to be like the other lads I worked with, so when they bought leather jackets, so did I. However, the jacket I bought was way too big for me and I must have looked ridiculous.

Finally, though, I was ready to enter the club. Preparing to walk through the doors into the main room, the excitement was immense. In my mind I felt like Mike Tyson about to walk out into a huge arena and make his way to the ring for a world championship fight. The reality was I was just a nobody walking into a club for the first time ever, and nobody gave a shit.

I had planned that whole experience in my head for so long, convinced it was going to be the best night ever. But actually, I can barely remember a thing. I was with work friends at the start of the night, but can't remember if they got into the club with me or if I ended up with different people. I do, however, remember seeing my sister, who was shocked I'd actually managed to get in.

At one point, I was standing talking to one of my sister's friends next to a pillar with mirrors all around it. I don't know who it was or why they did this, but someone walked past me and pushed my head hard, smacking it into the mirror. I tried to look around for who it was, but the place was busy, and I couldn't really see straight by that point. It was probably someone I'd tried to fight in town a few weeks earlier. Back then I was pretty good at starting fights. I was a gobby little asshole once I'd had a drink, but didn't have the first clue when it came to actual fighting. On most occasions I either left my mates to deal with the fallout or I got knocked out.

That night, not long after my head hit the pillar, I blacked out. The next thing I remember is waking up, still in the club, sitting on a chair near the edge of the dance floor, music blaring. For some reason, I only had my boxer shorts on! Wondering what the fuck had happened, I began scrabbling around on the floor for my clothes. After a few minutes, I managed to find my trousers and put them back on. I searched around for more of my clothes but couldn't find any, so I decided just my trousers would be sufficient.

I really badly needed to go to the toilet, so I tried to work out where I was and which way it was to get to the gents. There were a few stairs you had to go up that led to another bigger staircase, and the toilets were up there. I stood up somehow, and started walking across to the stairs. There was a line of people on the smaller set of stairs, so I tried to signal to them that I wanted to get past, but they wouldn't move.

I tried to shout, 'Excuse me!' but when they still wouldn't move I decided I would need to just force my way past them. It became a real battle of me trying to push them out the way.

All of a sudden, the music stopped.

At that moment, I realised I was in my bedroom at home, and I was attempting to walk through my wall. I have no idea how I'd managed to get home, but the first thought that entered my head was delight that I didn't have to try and make it up some stairs to get to a toilet. I stumbled out of my bedroom, but turned the wrong way and actually stood in the hallway and urinated on my sister's bedroom door. I had no idea I'd done this at the time, but my sister reminded me years later. And even when she told me about it, I didn't remember doing it.

Most people reading this might think that was a funny story and that no real harm was done. At the time I didn't really care too much about it either. I thought it was great that I had somehow managed to get home, and it seemed like a normal thing to happen. I used to think a blackout from drinking was just what happened when you had a good night out. I'd had them before when I was drinking, although this was the first time I'd managed to get into a club.

But the whole incident is actually quite frightening, because I have no memory at all of how I left the club or how I got home. Anything could have happened to me, and it should have terrified me that I'd been so drunk that I'd missed most of the night and had no recollection of how I got home. But I just brushed it off like it was nothing.

I'm not saying everyone that has a blackout through drinking is an alcoholic. But looking back now, I can see all the signs of it within me. I didn't see them at the time, but it's as clear as day now. The excitement all day that we would be out that night. The rush to get home and change so I could get back out as quickly as possible. The stress about whether I would get served in some of the pubs. The anxiety of not getting into the club and the night being cut short. Once I'd started drinking, the complete inability to stop. Getting so drunk I had no memory of what happened.

Some people do this kind of thing for a short period of their life then grow out of. When responsibilities come along, they sort themselves out. And that is great; good on them. I know a lot of people who have done that, but it's still scary how often as youngsters we managed to put ourselves into really dangerous situations because we all believed that going out and getting blind drunk was a normal thing to do. Let me tell you, there is nothing normal about having a blackout.

What stands out the most for me about this story, though, is the fact that the next day I did not care one bit about what had happened. I just nursed a hangover, probably by going out later in the day and having a hair of the dog. That was always my method: just start again, and get rid of the headache.

During that period, nothing in my life mattered except alcohol. I had a job to pay for the drink, but even that wasn't really important; if I lost a job, I'd just go and get another one. It wasn't always that easy, but I was never really out of work for long. I must have been really good at interviews because people always seemed willing to employ me.

Some people have this idea that to be an alcoholic you have to drink every day, or start first thing in the morning. And there were certainly some periods when I did drink every day. But even when I didn't, I was still an alcoholic. Looking back, I can see that I was either drinking or I was thinking about drinking. So even on a sober day, I was still a slave to the booze, because I was thinking about how I could make an excuse to go and have a drink.

That period of my life, and the nightclub incident, remind me of this concept. I worked a minimum wage job for six days a week to fund my habit. I didn't earn enough, so I was dishonest and stole money so that I could afford to drink more often. I lived at home with my parents, and very often

I didn't pay the rent I was supposed to because I spent all my money on alcohol. I was horrible to my parents and often created arguments with my mum for no reason, just because I was drunk. I think I used my parents as my excuse for the way I behaved for a long time, and it was a couple of years into recovery before I worked out that it wasn't their fault. I had absolutely no ambition in my life other than to drink. No career plans, no thought of education, no desire to get on the property ladder.

I remember around this time, one of my closest friends was getting ready to go to university, and I actually thought he was a bit of a loser. I couldn't understand why anyone would want to go to university. He's the one laughing now, though, with a highly paid job and a happy family.

For years, while I was behaving this way, I always had someone to blame. Every time something went wrong in my life, I had no ability to look in the mirror and see that I was the one who had caused it. And I could never put two and two together and see that alcohol was always at the centre of everything.

The truth is that nobody else was to blame; I was just looking for excuses. And I can also see now that the real me wasn't to blame either. The disease of addiction was the problem, but I had no idea what that meant back then. Nowadays, there is a lot of information available about addiction, what it is, and what can cause it. But there wasn't at that time, and I certainly didn't know it was something I was suffering with.

Now, with several years of experience as an active addict and a few extra years as a recovering addict, I have built up quite a wealth of knowledge on the subject, and I think we need to go over what addiction is before we go any further into my story. This isn't anything proven scientifically or studied by a professor; these are just my thoughts and my 40 years of living with the issue. I'm going to give you my opinion of what addiction is, based on my years of lived experience. And I believe that learning about something from someone who has lived experience is always much better than reading from a textbook.

Chapter 2
The disease of addiction

The biggest misconception when it comes to addiction is that it only applies to drugs. Some people still have a difficult time associating alcohol with addiction unless it's the bottom-end alcoholic, living on the streets, drinking every day. And most people look down at what's below them as a problem, as it allows them to feel better about anything they do. I used to be snorting hundreds of pounds worth of cocaine up my nose daily while looking down on a heroin addict because he injected his drugs. I was walking around thinking I was somehow a much more high-end, classy drug user. Bullshit! I just basically justified what I was doing because someone else was doing it much worse than I was.

Another thing people get wrong with addiction is the idea that you only become addicted to some form of chemical substance that you are putting into your body, whether that's alcohol or illegal drugs. Sometimes it *is* the substance, but most of the time it is the actual effects that become addictive.

For me, **addiction is fixing how I feel by using anything outside of me**. For most addicts this ends up being in the form of a drink or a drug. I wasn't happy with the way my life was going, and I wanted to feel different. And the instant sensation I got from a drink made me feel better, so I kept wanting more and more. Alcoholism and drug addiction are a little different. When we start drinking or using drugs, it sets off a craving inside of us that we cannot switch off, and we just want more and more until we pass out. You might remember from the story in Chapter 1 that I lost the ability to stop once I had started.

People can also become addicted to things that are not chemicals, but which still change the way we feel. You probably know a lot of these but don't associate them with addiction: sex, gambling, food, work, shopping, exercise, to name a few. They can also change how we feel and give us that dopamine hit, and they can be just as addictive. However, people can suffer with an addiction to some of these vices and get away with it their whole life, because it isn't as outwardly destructive as being addicted to drink and drugs. I'm not in any way saying these addictions are not serious or can't lead to major problems. If you have a gambling problem, for instance, it can still ruin your life with the amount of money you could lose. But it doesn't become a noticeable problem as quickly as drink and drug addiction does.

And another type of addiction that isn't always highlighted is when people take certain drugs and it isn't the chemical of the drug that is addictive. I've met people who take steroids or inject a tan to alter the pigmentation of their skin, so they appear to have a tan without going out in the sun or on sunbeds. In these cases, it's not the chemicals that have them hooked; it's the results they see on how their body looks that is addictive. The drug changes the way they look, and they become addicted to the feeling they have from looking better. Personally, I don't think it's a better look, but the people that do it clearly like it. A guy I know does it far too much, and I don't think he even has an end goal, like, 'When I get to this big, I'll stop,' or 'When my skin is this dark, I'll stop.' He just keeps going. I don't know the full health dangers doing this to extreme can cause, but I imagine it isn't good for you.

I genuinely believe that every person on this planet is on the addiction scale somewhere, but we all have different intensities of how much we want to change how we feel, and we all have different vices that give us the dopamine hit we crave. Unfortunately, the society we live in now, with the technology available, is only making this more prevalent. Just look at how social media has made everyone so anti-social, endlessly scrolling through their newsfeed, searching for the next bit of gossip or thing to be offended by. These platforms are designed by psychologists to get you hooked on the infinite scroll, so you keep going. How many times have you been looking through your feed and, before you know it, hours have passed? I know I'm guilty of it myself sometimes. We used to have to pick up the phone or actually walk to see our friends and find out what they were up to, but now we just check their socials and message them if we see something we want to talk to them about.

People get away with some forms of addiction because the vice they use to fix how they feel isn't so destructive. If I'm feeling a little bit down and decide to buy a new pair of trainers, I get the instant hit that makes me feel better. But it doesn't set off a craving inside me to go and buy another 50 pairs in one day. I might have bought two pairs in one day, but with shopping there is usually an off switch. Others who get addicted to work usually become very successful and probably earn quite a bit of money. But this could lead to an addiction to gambling because they have spare cash and can afford to. Or it could damage their family dynamic because they are always too busy to spend quality time with their loved ones.

So, I believe that we are all addicts, just with different vices and different intensities of our addiction. You could have two people who both use biscuits as their go-to when they feel low. One of them may open a packet and eat 3-4 biscuits and feel better, then put them away. The other person may not be able to stop once they start, smash the whole packet, then feel awful for eating so much. They have both used something outside of themselves to fix how they feel, but just at vastly different levels.

In a way, I'm glad that my vice for such a long time was drink and then drugs. Because it is such a destructive form of addiction that it becomes clear to everyone around you that there is a problem. And then, slowly but surely, I was forced to realise that something wasn't right, and it made me look at my behaviour and to do something about it. Now that I know what is wrong with me, I've been able to learn so much about myself and about the disease of addiction, so I can continuously monitor my behaviour. I have to do this for many reasons, but mostly it is to make sure that I am not hurting other people, and I'm keeping an eye out for early signs of a relapse.

I have discovered that my addiction falls into the category of the highest intensity. If I'm using a vice to fix how I feel, there is a very high chance that I'm going to take it to the extreme. I know this because, if I look back on my life, I've had these addictive patterns of behaviour since childhood – a long time before I even picked up a drink or took a drug.

When I say there are people with lower intensities, I mean someone who perhaps has a stressful job and every night goes home, sits down with a large glass of wine, and instantly feels better. Then they put the bottle away and don't touch another drop until they get home the following day. I am born with high intensity addiction, but I would consider the person who drinks one glass of wine a day a low intensity addict. Yes, they have used something to fix how they feel, but they keep it to a manageable level.

Now imagine if something traumatic happened to that person. Three of the biggest traumas people can experience are: losing your job, a relationship breakdown, and a family bereavement. All of these experiences can be out of your control. If a person experiences one or more of these events, there is a high chance they might then start using their vice more often to cope with their feelings around that trauma. One glass becomes a bottle a night, then two bottles a night. Then they lose their job because they're drinking too much. The point I'm making is that it doesn't matter what level of addiction you are born with, there could be an incident or circumstance in your life that causes you to change the amount you use your vice and it develops into a higher, more destructive level. **Everybody is one traumatic experience away from addiction.**

A good description of addiction I once read was, "I always feel irritable, restless, and discontented." This perfectly describes the way I used to feel for as long as I can remember. When I first got into recovery, I didn't know what the sentence really meant, but I think in my case it meant angry, bored, and never satisfied. When I was around four or five years old, my mum would take us to the big supermarket to do the weekly shopping, and at the time I was big into He-Man. The store had a huge display of He-Man action figures in the toy section, and every week we would go and pick out one that I wanted. I would feel such excitement on the way to the shop, knowing I would be getting a new toy, and trying to decide which one I wanted. And I couldn't wait to get out of the shop and head home so that I could open it and start playing. But within a day, it was just another toy to add to the collection. That one wasn't enough, and I wanted more. Nothing was ever enough – toys, TV, sweets. I was never satisfied.

Over the years in recovery, you get to talk to a lot of other alcoholics and addicts, and one of the subjects we always discuss is whether we remember our first drink. I can remember mine, and the story is ridiculous. I was born in Coventry and lived there with my parents and two sisters. But a lot of factories in the Midlands were closing in the late eighties, which meant there was less work available. When my dad managed to find a job down in Devon, my parents made the decision to relocate to the south-west. I think I was five years old at the time, but can't remember exactly. I'm starting to think I might need to get dates and times from my family, because my memory is so bad.

The night before the removal vans turned up for the move, my parents were having a big leaving party. I remember there being a table full of drinks in the kitchen, but being so young I didn't know what a lot of them were. I knew what a can of lager was, because my dad usually had one in his hands when he wasn't working. However, that night I took a liking to the bottle that had a picture of a bird on the side, and I started having a few sips of it every time I went into the kitchen. Little did I know that it was a big bottle of Woodpecker cider. According to reports from others, I went missing for ages. The adults were looking for me for a while, then someone found me under the table in the kitchen, hidden by the tablecloth, looking very confused. I apparently had the bottle of cider in my hands, trying to drink it with the lid still on, wondering why nothing was coming out.

I don't have a massive recollection of this happening. I remember the start of the night, but I don't remember how it ended. Was that my first ever blackout? Who knows? I only know about what happened because it became a sort of legendary tale that was shared by my parents for years because everyone found it so funny. To a lot of people, the story of a five-year-old sitting under a kitchen table so drunk they can't open a bottle would be quite a horrifying tale. But my family found it quite funny and were never shy about telling people what had happened. Now that I don't drink, if it had happened to one of my children, I'm not sure I would have the same attitude towards such a story. I would more than likely want to keep that one to myself. But I try not to do other people's thinking for them; my parents have their reasons for finding that story funny, and I won't take that away from them.

That is the story of my first drink, but obviously I didn't become an alcoholic right there and then. I wasn't screaming at my mum for a whisky instead of a juice or knocking back shots with my old man. But the story tells me a lot about why I believe I was born with a high intensity level of addiction. I hadn't gone into the kitchen to look for an alcoholic drink that night, and it was purely by chance that I liked the picture of the bird and picked up the cider. I can't imagine cider tasted very appealing to a five-year-old, so you would normally expect that one sip would be enough and I would then look for something else. Yet I kept going back for more. Was this because I liked it, or was this the first time I had a sense of the craving in my head? I didn't want to stop, I kept going back, and it's been the same since I became an adult – once I've started, I cannot stop. I also have no memory of the end of that night. Was that because I was just very young and I don't have many early memories? Or was that the first time I blacked out from alcohol?

Of course, I'm not saying that night was the starting point of my addiction, nor am I blaming my parents for what happened. But knowing what I do now about addiction, I can look back and see that from an early age, long before I was legally old enough to drink, I was already showing addictive behaviour when it came to alcohol. And it was the same behaviour when it came to other things that would fix how I felt.

I read something in some recovery literature that described me perfectly, but sadly can't give the author any credit because I have forgotten where I read it:

I have a God-shaped hole,

For most of my life I have felt an emptiness in my core. As a child I tried to fill this emptiness with constant TV watching or by pigging out on candy. When I discovered alcohol and drugs, I devoured both, trying to fill the void I felt. When I began my professional career, I used the money I made to fill the hole by buying cars, clothes, and other material items. The horrible thing is that nothing worked. No matter how much I ate or drank or bought, the desperate feeling of emptiness never went away.

When I entered recovery, I began hearing others talk about a similar hole they felt as well. I heard familiar tales of obsessive use and abuse of alcohol and other things, all in an attempt to fill that hole. No matter how much or in what combination they tried, nothing worked. Everyone still felt irritable, restless, and discontented. I heard many people say they felt like others were given the operating manual to life but they didn't get one. I felt that same way for most of my life, too.

As I made my way through the Twelve Steps, my feeling of emptiness began to subside. The deeper into the journey I went, the more my hole seemed to get filled. The closer I got to my Higher Power, the more centered and fulfilled I became. As I talked to others about this, I was told that all my life I had a God-shaped hole, and that I had been trying to fill it with the wrong things. Only a surrender and connection to God could ever fill the emptiness I felt. As I poured His love and light into my life, I felt whole for the first time.

Today I know that I have a God-shaped hole, and only continued conscious contact will keep me whole and happy.

Author, Unknown

If you read that quote and started thinking I'm about to go off on a religious rant and try to convert you to God, then believe me when I say I'm not a religious person at all… but I believe in spirituality. However, that's irrelevant. The point is that I identify with the above passage in that I spent all my life trying to fill the void in me with the wrong things, and no matter how much I tried it was never good enough.

So now ask yourself: do you use things outside of you to fix how you feel? Does it give you the hit of dopamine that you enjoy? Do you sometimes lose control of how much you're using, whichever vice you've chosen? Can you place yourself on that addiction scale somewhere?

I'm not saying being on the addiction scale means we're all going to become bottom-end, alcoholic drug addicts living on the streets. But if you're on the scale and you acknowledge it, the situation becomes much easier to monitor and do something about. The main reason people suffer with addiction is because of the denial that comes along with it. Believing that there was nothing wrong with me and that everything was someone else's fault is what kept me living in active addiction for so long.

Addiction is a disease that tells me I don't have it.

Chapter 3

Addiction is environmental?

There are a lot of arguments that the environment you are brought up in can determine whether you become an addict. Some of these I agree with, and some I don't. I'm no scientist, and I've done no studies, but I have a lot of first-hand knowledge that I can share with you.

You may say that someone who lives in a lower class of society is more prone to becoming an addict, mainly because their situation is more visible to others every day. But perhaps stop and think that the reason you see it more often is because there are a lot more people these days living in lower social classes. So, just by basic maths, there will be more addicts in that environment. Also, a lot of addicts in the upper classes probably manage to hide their issues from the public view much better. How many times do you see a news story about an A-list celebrity admitting he has a drink problem, yet nobody in the public eye had a clue about it because that person managed to keep it hidden behind closed doors?

I'm not saying that environment plays *no* part. I'm sure it is a factor in some ways. But I still believe in my theory that all people are born with addictive tendencies – just at very different levels of intensity. The environment you are in could cause your intensity of addiction to change over a period of time, in just the same way that it could be affected by some sort of trauma. Maybe environmental factors would make it a much more progressive change.

How we change in our addiction is very much on an individual basis. I mean, if someone is abused as a child, then they grow up using drink and drugs to cope and become an addict, you could look at that scenario and say it was the abuse that made him or her that way. But then surely if that was the case, every single person who was abused as a child would become an addict. And while I don't have statistics, we all know that's not the case.

More importantly, addiction does not discriminate. You see addicts from all walks of life, and you also see non-addicts from all social backgrounds, too. That is why I think that how we progress in addiction is based on the individual and how they react to different situations. I've met addicts that have terrible stories of trauma from their childhood. And I also know some addicts who say they had a perfect childhood and admit they have no excuse for it. But we don't need an excuse. If we are born with a high-level intensity of addiction, then that's the hand we are dealt. And the only solution is to realise quickly that this is the problem, become aware of it, and learn what we can do about it.

You could also look at addiction in the same way as people now do with depression. We see celebrities who appear from the outside to have everything you could wish for, yet they feel so low with depression that they take their own lives. You don't need to be poor and living in the lowest class of society to suffer with depression and feel like death is the only way out. It happens to wealthy, successful people, too. So why can't addiction be the same? People from all environments suffer with addiction. Some turn it round and some don't, but again, that is to do with the individual and not their environment.

Another reason why I believe in the illness being more about the individual is the fact that I have two older sisters, and neither of them is the same as me when it comes to drink or drugs. Yet we were all brought up in the same house by the same parents. Somehow my genetics were different to my siblings, and I became the addict/alcoholic. I've had conversations with one of my sisters about this, and she is the kind of person I mentioned earlier that can come home from work, have one glass of wine, then put the bottle away and not drink any more. She has still used the wine to alter the way she feels, but it just hasn't set off the craving that it would within me. She is the sister who was in the club that night I talked about in Chapter 1. In those days, she would go out most weekends with her mates and get pretty drunk, like I did, but one day she just seemed to grow out of it.

When we were growing up, the culture was very different when it came to alcohol. I can remember that most events, whether it was someone's birthday or wedding, usually ended with most of the family being at a party where drink was heavily involved. Even at weekends, most things we did as a family ended up with us being at the local pub. When I was quite young – I'm not sure how old – our parents told us that they were looking into leasing the pub round the corner from where we lived, and they asked how we would feel about living above it. I was nowhere near old enough to drink alcohol, but the excitement I felt about living above a pub was ridiculous. For weeks I was hoping and praying that they were going to go ahead with it. I was imagining how I would get loads of extra cool points at school because of it, and that everyone would want to be my best mate. So, when my parents broke the news that they weren't going to go through with it, I was devastated. Clearly, I was fascinated with that sort of lifestyle from a young age.

Another memory I clearly recall was that every other Friday evening at the local leisure centre, they used to hold what they called a Family Fun Night. Basically, there was a bar with a big function room next door, and they brought in a DJ and dancefloor for entertainment, and blew up a bouncy castle in the corner for the kids. It was a night put on for adults to get pissed, while the kids had somewhere to play. I'm not sure if that sort of thing still goes on now, but I can assure you it's the last thing I would want to take my children to. I'm not saying I didn't enjoy it; as a kid, I thought it was brilliant. We ran wild all night and stayed up later than normal. What's not to like? And again, I'm not saying these things contributed to me being an alcoholic, because my sisters went there, too, and they didn't turn out like me.

Since becoming sober, and looking back over my life at reasons why the addiction took over, I've realised that one huge factor during my teenage years was when I moved from middle school up to high school. I had always suffered from low self-esteem and just wanted to be liked by people, but the middle school I went to had two classrooms in our year, of around 30 kids in each, so no more than 60 in the whole year. When you move up to high school, suddenly you are in a year group of 300. It's a massive difference and a huge shock to the system. In the middle school, for some reason, I was seen as the hardest person in the year and had quite a lot of friends. The funny thing is that I don't even remember having a single fight while I was there, but somehow I managed to get a big, tough kid reputation, so I just rolled with it and tried to maintain it. Truth is, I was petrified of confrontation, so while I was walking round acting tough, I was praying nobody would really challenge me or I would have been exposed as a fraud.

When the time came to move up, the problem I faced was that only three people from our school went on to the same high school: me, one other boy, and a girl. The other boy, I can't even remember his name, got bullied badly and moved to a different school within about a month. The girl had an older sister in the school, so she had a friend circle in place already. I went from being the big fish in a year group of 60 to an absolute nobody in a group of 300 kids. The others all had their friend groups in place from their middle schools, and I didn't know anyone. Looking back now, I realise how alone I felt once I'd got there. But again, I just tried to hide my feelings and fit in as best I could.

For the first couple of years of high school, I knuckled down and focussed on the work. I saw that as my top priority. If I couldn't make friends, at least I could be good in class, because I was seen as quite a clever kid.

And I did try my best to fit in with different groups of kids. I often describe it as I would wake up, pick which bullshit suit I was going to put on that day, then head into school and try to fit in with that group. I loved football but wasn't good enough, so didn't fit in with that group. I tried to get in with the gamer kids, but I wasn't massive into consoles and never really had any of my own to learn on. I tried to get in with a group who were into mountain biking, but I felt inferior because the bike I had was shit, and they had spent thousands on theirs. Looking back, I think at times I did have friend groups, but I more than likely didn't feel like I was being accepted so decided to move away from those people.

Speaking to people from high school now, they seem to remember me as being quite popular and very confident when I was there. But that isn't how I ever saw it; I always felt like a loner, just getting by. That was until I found myself getting friendly with the rebellious group who would sneak out at lunchtimes, smoke cigarettes on the school field, and go drinking down the park at the weekends. All of a sudden, I had found a group of people that I really did fit in with.

As you know, I'd always been fascinated with alcohol. Drinking was normal and something I'd seen people doing while I was growing up, so I always knew it was only a matter of time before I would start myself – a case of when I would start, not if. As soon as I found out people my age were meeting up down at the park by the river with bottles of cheap cider and a pack of 10 Larry and Barrys (Lambert and Butler, for anyone who wasn't born in the 80s), I was trying my best to get an invite to join them.

Finally, not only had I found a group of people doing something I could enjoy, but I discovered I was really bloody good at it, too. At last I was being praised for being the best at something. It became a bit of a running joke in my new circle of friends that there wasn't anybody that could keep up with me when it came to the booze. I also found that when I started drinking alcohol with all the kids from school, it acted as an instant anxiety remover. Alcohol gave me the confidence I had been craving to do all the things I wanted to do. I could act like the joker and feel popular. I could talk to the girls I fancied without feeling stupid. It seemed to take away all the problems I thought I had in my life. I often talk to people about how odd this period was. I would have a girlfriend and be all confident with her at the weekend when I'd been drinking, but during the week when we were back at school, I was too shy to even talk to her.

It was around that time that my focus on everything changed. I lost all ambition in school; in fact, I hardly ever attended for most of my last year. My only goal at that point was to find ways of getting money and people that would buy me the alcohol. There wasn't a shortage of ways to get cash as I'd had a good work ethic from a young age, working part-time at weekends. And there wasn't a shortage of people where I lived who were old enough to get the drink for us.

I suppose you could argue that a lot of the environments or situations I found myself in while I was developing from a child to an adult could have been a huge factor in me becoming an alcoholic. But I still disagree. I firmly believe I was born with an addictive nature of the higher intensity that I described earlier. Of course, the people and places I encountered while I was growing up possibly helped me to develop my addiction quicker. But I was always going to drink; I knew it way before I started. And with a real alcoholic head that has the craving, once they start, that is what was always going to happen.

The proof of my argument is the fact that my sisters grew up to be very different to me – even though they grew up in the same house, with the same parents, and went to the same school. They show addictive traits, but of a very low intensity, so it doesn't become an issue for them in everyday life.

It's funny, though, because quite a lot of the people I grew up with in that area did develop drink and drug problems. It's not up to me to diagnose whether any of them are alcoholics, though; it's up to them whether they believe that to be the case. But for a small area, there was certainly a lot of drinking going on, so you could say that the environment was a breeding ground for alcoholics. Or maybe it was just a rough area, and alcohol was the only escape for a lot of people.

Something else that grabs my attention now is how much we are programmed by mainstream media. Back in the 80s and 90s, you only had four TV channels. Every night on two of the four there was always a soap opera that basically told us that normal life was living in a rough area, always down the pub, having ding-dongs in the street over who had slept with whose wife. Back then it was the most popular thing on TV and attracted millions of viewers every night. So, in reality, were our real-life environments being shaped for us by subconsciously being brainwashed into thinking that what we watched on TV was normal? Was it our environment, or one that was created for us?

Either way, it makes no difference to me. I stand by my theory that everybody is on the addiction scale from birth, but we all just start with different levels of intensity. Environments can alter this intensity slowly. Trauma can change the intensity quicker. And the substance or vice can be anything we choose. It doesn't always have to lead to becoming a low-bottom alcoholic or drug addict. The difference is that when an alcoholic brain slips down the addiction scale and takes the first drink or drug, it sets off that craving in the brain. And that is when you see the marked difference between someone like me and someone who might eat a few too many biscuits now and then.

Chapter 4

Always a step too far

A common theme when I started drinking was the fact that quite often I would be the one who took it too far and ended up making very bad decisions. It would usually end with me upsetting people or getting myself into trouble – or both. The reason behind this is that as soon as an alcoholic has that first drink, it sets off the craving that we want more. Then on top of that, we have the complete inability to stop.

The baffling thing was that there was no rhyme or reason as to how a night would end once I started drinking. Some nights I would drink in moderation. Sometimes I would drink too much to the point of blackout but remain in a good mood and just be a happy, jolly drunk. Other times would be blackout, and I would turn into a nasty, horrible, and sometimes violent drunk. I know now that once I start, I don't have the ability to choose how it's going to end. If I could, I would always choose to drink in moderation and be in a happy, tipsy kind of state. But as that only happens on a handful of occasions, I can see clearly that I cannot make the choice of how it ends.

Of course, I couldn't see that when I was still drinking; it's only something I've learned since finding recovery. What used to happen when I drank was that I would show unacceptable kinds of behaviour but also try to justify them.

It's quite embarrassing really to think back to some of these events.

I'll give you a funny story first before going into a real cringe one. At my sister's 18th birthday party, I'd been drinking quite a lot. I think I was about 15 or 16 at the time, and my best friend from school had come along with us. Part-way through the evening, I was on the dance floor trying to throw some shapes and maybe impress my sister's female friends. The song *The Time Warp* came on – the old caravan holiday park classic with its own set of dance moves. There were two lines of people facing each other on the dance floor, but for some reason I decided to take up position in the middle of the two lines, right at the end, like I was head of a huge dinner table-type formation. What I didn't realise was that someone was at the other end of the two lines with a camcorder videotaping the dance. So, on the tape all you can see is a line of people each side of the screen and then just me at the other end. In the song, there is a bit where they say "jump to the left" and everyone jumps left. And then "step to the right", and everyone steps to the right. When the song got to that part and everyone jumped left, I tried to jump left but couldn't stop myself, and kept going left, stumbling along after the landing. So, on the video all you see is me jump left, land, stumble, and then end up on my ass on the floor.

This video was kept for years and, just like the leaving party story of me ending up drunk under the table, this became like a legendary family event. I lost count of the number of times this video was taken out and put on for people to watch, and everyone found it hilarious the state I'd got into. I used to laugh along, too, but I cringe when I think back to it now. I have no idea what happened to the video, but I hope it's lost forever. If it's ever found, I'll transfer it from old VHS tape onto computer and charge a fee for people to watch it online.

That, though, was a mild night for me. Most of the times when I took things too far I just became a gobby, aggressive, little asshole. I would usually end up drinking to the point of being sick, and getting in trouble sometimes with this, too. One night, while I was still living with my parents, I had been out and came home really drunk. I'd got myself off to bed but had that stomach-wrenching, watery-mouth feeling, along with that burning sensation in the back of the throat like acid reflux. I knew I was about to be sick, but I knew there was no way I would make it to the bathroom. So, I stood up on my bed and puked out of the window into the back garden. I thought in my head that I'd just go and clean it in the morning and nobody would ever know. But that didn't go to plan.

The next morning, I woke up to the sound of my dad shouting in the kitchen, "That dirty little bastard!" and a few other choice words to describe me. What I hadn't realised was that for some unknown reason he had put his hard hat and work boots out on the back step when he got home from work the night before, and both were now filled with my vomit. Not a good start to the day for him at all. I stayed upstairs out of the way and tried to avoid him for days. I don't remember getting too much of a hard time from him, though; I think they had got used to my behaviour by that point.

At my cousin's funeral, I tried to fight one of my other cousins because he'd called my late nan a bitch, and I loved her very much. I think I was only about 14 at the time, completely smashed, and the guy I was trying to fight was a fully grown man who worked as a prison officer. Luckily, my uncles saved me from getting my ass kicked.

Another time, we were at my other cousin's wedding, and it was right at the end of the night when most people were getting ready to leave. I was wobbling around drunk when a pint glass that was on the floor got knocked over while someone was walking past, and it hit my foot. I looked up, decided who it was that had knocked it towards me, and kicked the glass as hard as I could towards him. The glass smacked into the back of his foot really hard. Obviously, he wasn't too pleased about this and came over to ask me why I'd done it, and a fight was about to break out. Lots of family members all came rushing over to break us up, but all the while I was screaming, blaming him, saying he had kicked the glass at me first. Basically, I can look at it now and say that I was drunk and angry. I made a bad choice to kick the glass at someone and then tried to justify my stupid decision. I still need to make amends for that little drama.

Those are just a few stories I can remember, but this book would be way too long if I reeled off all of them, and you'd get bored. I have to give you one more, because this is the most cringeworthy I can remember. It was Nan and Grandad's ruby wedding anniversary, I think – or one that was quite important – so the whole family had arranged to be at this fancy hotel to celebrate and give them gifts. I think it was quite early in the day, so I'm not sure why I was already so drunk.

My cousins were there, and they lived next door to a girl I had the hots for. We'd met at a party at my aunty and uncle's house a few months before and got a little bit intimate, so I'd asked my cousin for her phone number. This was back when mobile phones were quite a new thing, and having people's phone number wasn't as common as it is now. So, while literally the whole of my dad's side of the family were sitting in this function room waiting for food to be served, I decided it would be a good time to phone this young lady. I expect I was showing off a bit that I had a mobile phone.

The girl answered the phone, and we chatted a bit, but she was with a group of male friends who started shouting things to me. I'm not even sure what they were shouting, but they were obviously trying to wind me up. So, I began raising my voice at the girl, saying things like "Who the fuck are they? Who do they think they are?" Eventually she put one of them on the phone and I went in with the big hard man act, screaming down the phone at him, challenging him to come to my hometown and I'd smash him to pieces. I was using language that was just disgusting in front of family, and I think I dropped the C-bomb in there quite a few times. It must have gone on for a good 5-10 minutes, just me shouting all kinds of profanities at these random people, and by the end I could feel everyone in the room had stopped whatever they were doing and were all focused on me.

I put the phone down, but I was still fuming. I looked up and everyone was staring at me, completely shocked at what they had just witnessed. What's crazy about this is that I was expecting everyone to stand up and start cheering and clapping for what a mighty display of male dominance I'd just shown. I felt like I was a hero and had absolutely no idea why everyone was pissed off with me or why my immediate family felt a massive sense of embarrassment. Why wouldn't everyone be proud of what I had just done? There was no way I was going to let people speak down to me. Who did they think they were?

There I was, casually trying to once more justify really shitty behaviour. But I can remember the look on my mum's face as she looked across at me from another table, mouth wide open, almost as though her jaw was literally on the floor. Yet I really didn't understand what I'd done wrong; I thought I was perfectly within my rights to behave like that. I always say to people that I used to have this fantasy that I could just behave like a wild rockstar, except that I never learned how to play an instrument. I used to think that someone would come along one day and pay me millions just for being a complete legend. But I had absolutely no talent that was worth the millions I wanted.

Friends and family would tell me quite often, "You're lovely when you're sober. Why can't you just have a couple and then stop?" And the honest answer was, I had no idea.

Back then, I was unaware of what happens to an alcoholic as soon as you put a drink in them. I didn't understand how the craving for more starts, that the off switch becomes stuck, and how we lose the ability to moderate or control the amount we are going to consume. At one point in my drinking, I tried to work out which drink it was that tipped me over the edge. I sat in a bar counting the amount of drinks I'd had and took mental notes of how I was reacting, trying to work out exactly which one sent me over the edge. But there is no set amount. For an alcoholic, one is too many and 100 isn't enough.

At this point, hopefully you can start to see the differences between people who use vices in an addictive way but only mildly, and someone who is an alcoholic type of addict. People who use different vices to change how they feel, like shopping or fitness training, can get away with drinking alcohol because their brains don't have that same craving as an alcoholic does. And they can moderate their drinking, unlike us. So, people can be on the addiction scale but not take things to the extreme like alcoholics do. Once *we* start, there is no off switch.

Alcohol changes the behaviour of most people, and we all do things that we would normally find unacceptable. But the alcoholic tends to go that one step further because of that lack of ability to stop drinking once they've started.

This is one of the reasons that I couldn't see there was an issue for so long. I was going out on a regular basis with people doing the same thing as me. We were all getting drunk and getting ourselves into trouble. So I thought it was normal. The problem was, they could stop at a certain point, but usually it was me going that one step too far.

When we use something like working or shopping as a vice, we get the initial dopamine fix that we are looking for to make ourselves feel better in that moment, but there isn't a chemical element in the vice that changes the brain's chemistry. If we add a substance like alcohol or cocaine into our body to fix how we feel, this starts kicking off the alcoholic tendencies, like the craving and the inability to stop. This is why people who are only slightly on the addiction scale can get away with drinking alcohol. They use it to alter the way they feel and get the instant relief they crave, but it doesn't make them want more and more the way an alcoholic does.

I'm no expert, but I'm pretty sure there could be a similar process when it comes to food addictions. You have Person A who uses a bit of cake to feel good when they are a bit low. They start to feel better but realise cake isn't too good for them, so they stop after one cake. Person B does the same, but then the signals that the sugary goodness sends to the brain kicks off the urge to eat more. Then they keep eating more and more – different food items, chocolate, biscuits, etc. I honestly believe there must be something contained within processed foods that causes some people to keep on eating until they can't physically eat any more. After their massive food binge, they probably feel a sense of shame and disgust at themselves for consuming so much crap, knowing that they are doing some real damage to their body. They will vow to never do it again and really mean it. Then when something is making them feel sad, a little voice in the back of their mind will be saying, "Go on, eat some cake. You know you'll feel better," and they will have forgotten how it ended last time and dive straight into the cake tin and start the process all over again. They probably tell themselves when they go shopping that they won't buy any of the treats they normally do, to make sure they don't have them in the house, but they cave in and buy a few. That makes it harder to stop themselves when they feel low.

People who don't behave this way around food would look at a person who is morbidly obese and ask themselves, "Why can't they just eat less unhealthy food and eat more salad?" To them, it seems like a simple enough question, but Person B would just say they don't know why they can't stop eating rubbish.

Now replace cake with alcohol, and you'll see that it is exactly the same problem. Firstly, I want to fix how I feel, and the quickest, easiest way I know how to is to have a drink. It's cheap, easily accessible, and I know it works in an instant. The average person – like my sister – can have the one drink, feel better, and then go on about their day. But not me. Once I've put one in me, that sets off that craving which I can only describe as feeling like a starving dog in my head that's screaming for more. So, I have another... and another. And I convince myself that I'll stop before I get out of control. But I don't realise that the first one has broken my off switch and I no longer have the ability to make myself stop.

So, it happens again. I black out and forget what I've done. Probably caused some trouble and upset some people. Wake up full of shame and remorse and swear to myself I'll never do it again. Then a few days later, I'm feeling low again and that voice in my head says, "Have a drink, Stewart, it will be fine." And I totally forget what happened a few days earlier. No matter how bad the consequences from the last time I had a drink, it doesn't stop me starting the same process again.

Sometimes, even loved ones in our lives can't see the problem either. I remember a few years ago the mother of my children would message me and ask if she should pick me up from work and we could take the kids for dinner in the pub. (This relationship also broke down, and we are not together any more.) I would agree to this, and when we got there, I'd have a pint with my dinner. Then I would say I'd go and order dessert, but I'd come back with another pint instead of choosing a pudding. So, by that stage I'd have had two, then on leaving I'd ask to go to the shop on the way home to get some cans. She would say, "No. Why do you need any more?"

This would cause me to feel hard done by, and I would sulk until I got my own way and got more beer to take home. Or I would create an argument so that I could have a tantrum and head to the pub, blaming her for being mean to me.

So, even though this person lived with me and saw on a regular basis what happened when I drank, they still didn't realise that one was too many and just started off the same cycle of events.

The next time you're with a friend or loved one and you're thinking, "You're obese, why can't you stop eating?" or,

"You're massively in debt, why can't you stop gambling?" think back to this. It's not the person's fault that they always take things a step too far. It's the disease of addiction that makes them unable to moderate and control their particular vice.

Chapter 5

A progressive illness

Something a lot of people don't understand about alcoholism is that it is a progressive illness. Once you have started drinking alcoholically, the beast you've awoken inside of you grows and gets worse. And even though at some points you think you are gaining some control, the reality is that any period of control is usually followed by even worse relapse. I didn't even know this myself, and I was living with it!

In my case, the denial just got stronger at the same time as the illness did. I tried to convince myself for years that I was in control, that I was choosing this way of life because I enjoyed it, and that at any given point I would decide the time was right to just calm down the partying and sort my life out. If I got the right job. If I got the perfect girlfriend. If I became a father.

Some of these events did happen, yet they still weren't enough to make me stop. And I still made myself think that it was my choice to continue.

Drinking started for me as though it was fairly normal behaviour; all my mates were doing almost the same as me. But near the end, it had reached a point where alcohol consumed me on a daily basis. I don't mean I was drinking every day or getting up and drinking first thing in the morning, but I was either drinking or I was thinking of a reason I could create to make it acceptable to drink. So, it was on my mind 24/7.

By the time I was legally old enough to drink, my problem was already out of control. But little did I know at the time that it was just the start of the progression.

In the early days, alcohol was enough for me. As I mentioned earlier, I used it to fix how I felt – the feeling of not fitting in, the insecurity, the anxiety, the depression. Alcohol took all that away in an instant. Taking that first drink, I could feel the relief flowing into me as I poured the liquid down my throat.

When I was just turning 18, all my mates were experimenting with drugs – ecstasy pills mainly – when we all went raving. I would go with them and just drink, but this caused problems as I would often pass out, and the people who were supposed to be giving us a lift home would refuse because of the state I was in.

I stuck with alcohol for a couple of reasons. Firstly, it was easy to access. I was old enough then and had legal ID, so if I wanted it, I would just go and buy it. And it was the quickest and easiest method to make myself feel good. On the other hand, getting drugs just seemed like a pain to me. You had to know who to get them from. Then make phone calls, and meet someone down a back alley, looking dodgy as hell. Then there was the risk of getting caught by the police. So, alcohol was legal and made the most sense to me. Secondly there were a few news stories around this time about young kids who had tried ecstasy for the first time and died, so that scared me a bit.

Eventually, though, peer pressure got the better of me, and I decided to give it a try. Well, it probably wasn't peer pressure, but more to do with the fact that drinking got me in a lot of trouble and the intrigue of trying something new, and probably with a stronger effect, gripped me. So, one night I gave it a try.

That night was actually really crazy. I ended up sitting with my next-door neighbour outside a block of flats near my house, doing nothing for hours. Just sitting there, looking around, seeing and hearing things that weren't really there, all tricks in my mind. We stayed there waiting for the effects to wear off so I could go home without my parents realising I was completely off my tits. But the feeling was amazing, and I was hooked. And that was the beginning of my relationship with drugs.

The next few years was a funny period. I would go through a few months of going mental with drink and drugs to the point where I was starting to lose everything. My parents would kick me out; I'd lose the girlfriend, if I had one at the time; I'd get sacked from whatever job I had. And I would see all of this going wrong and tell myself, "Come on, Stewart, you need to sort your life out!" My method to sort my life out was always to stop taking the drugs I was on and attempt to drink less alcohol. Giving up alcohol completely was never an option. I think because it was the only legal substance I was using, I sort of justified it as being ok.

Things would then somehow start looking up again for a while. I'd go and sweet talk my parents into letting me go home; I'd get a job somewhere; smarten myself up a bit again. Then once I was doing ok, I'd pat myself on the back and reward myself with a decent night out. I'd forget the damage I'd done before, and pretty soon I'd be back on drugs and drinking heavily again.

So when things went wrong, I was clearly smart enough to realise that drink and drugs were causing the problem and that I needed to rein them in to make any changes. But as soon as I was ok again, I just completely forget how bad I'd been. Alcoholism really is a disease of forgetfulness mixed with denial.

During this period, while getting fired from most jobs I'd been doing, I ended up working in the bar trade. It's no surprise that a lot of people I've met in recovery found themselves working in the hospitality industry – bar staff, chefs, hotel workers. I loved being in that environment, and getting paid to be there was a bonus. It was the perfect lifestyle for me, spending all day chatting with the customers having a drink, with me sneaking in the odd one myself here and there. And most nights when we finished work, everyone would go out to a nightclub. For about two years solid, I literally spent most days working hungover and then drunk afterwards. I got fired from a few pubs but just went and got employed at another one.

While working in one of the local bars, I met my first love. We got together and spent the first four months of our whirlwind relationship working together and then getting drunk. I'm not going to talk about our relationship at all, but the end result was she got pregnant very quickly. We agreed that having the baby would be a good idea, so we got a flat together and made a good go of becoming a family. This was one of those moments when I thought I would be the grown-up, decide I'd had enough of the party life, and that it was time to grow up and be a good father. But even when I had the best reason in the world to stop, I still couldn't.

I calmed down a little bit, but it was always just me playing games with my own mind, trying to convince myself that I was in control of my drinking. I went into a work mode where I thought I had to succeed to be a good provider for my family, but all I knew at the time was bar work, so I wanted to progress up to management level. I managed to get myself up to assistant manager of a busy high street pub that was part of a chain, and I hoped that they would give me a manager's job at one of their other pubs somewhere else in the country. But it never happened. Looking back now, I guess my boss and the area managers could see that I would have been a liability if I had been left to run my own pub.

After a year, my son's mother decided that she couldn't put up with my lifestyle any more. Always coming home drunk and making excuses. Not taking care of myself and looking rough all the time. Probably stinking because my personal hygiene was non-existent. She had the ability to grow up and become a great mother, but I was still in denial. At that point I still wasn't admitting to myself that I was an alcoholic. Everything that was going wrong for me was always someone else's fault, never mine, and not the alcohol.

One of the things I've realised is that the periods when I seemed to be not drinking as much, or as often as I would have liked, were usually when I was in a relationship and my partner didn't want me drinking so much. I would try to be a good boyfriend and attempt to limit my intake. But this also tricked me into thinking that I was controlling things, when in fact it was the relationship status that was making me seem more in control. When I was a single man, with nobody to try and impress, and I was doing my own thing, that was usually when my addictions got worse. And that is exactly what happened when my relationship with my son's mother ended.

I was a lone wolf again, doing my own thing, and I didn't have anyone that I needed to stay more sober for. Mixed with the heartbreak, I became even worse – drinking again, back on drugs, not caring who I hurt along the way, and being an even worse father than before. I used to look after my son sometimes, but I wasn't great at it. I would be there physically with him, but I would be somewhere else mentally – usually thinking about my next drink.

I spent the next couple of years going from job to job, and sofa to sofa. I was always getting kicked out by my parents and then finding a friend's house where I could stay until they had enough of me and kicked me out. I think I had a few material possessions, a bag of clothes, and nowhere to live, but I still thought I was doing ok.

During the periods when I was still trying to sort myself out, I kept going back to the bar trade because it was all I knew. I managed to get work in some of the pubs around town, but they were mainly the real rough, back-alley pubs where your feet would stick to the 20-year-old carpet that was soaked with a mixture of stale beer, sweat, and the blood of whoever had been fighting there recently.

In saying that, I felt like I fitted right in, but I suppose it's no surprise that an alcoholic ends up seeking out the really sordid places. The customers in there were drinking just the same as I was, so I could look down on them and think that I was nowhere near as bad as them. At that point, if you had taken me to a fancy cocktail bar, I would have felt really uncomfortable. Sit me in the back-alley pub where people were fighting most nights and I might be shit scared, but I certainly felt more at home there. I could sit with another alcoholic all night and talk complete bollocks, but it made me feel right at home.

On a few occasions I did manage to get jobs in better places. As I said earlier, I had a good ability to talk the talk brilliantly in an interview, so people would employ me. But the jobs never lasted very long. When I'd turn up drunk or hungover, or money went missing, the bosses would fire me pretty quickly. I was never caught stealing money from anywhere, but I think I was always suspected, so I would get fired for the first reason they could find instead.

I remember after I'd been sacked from one place where I'd worked, I bumped into another staff member a few weeks later. She mentioned that one of the managers had told her they couldn't understand why money was still going missing after they had got rid of me. When I told my family about this, I was outraged, saying I was going to beat the guy up if I saw him. So, in my head I thought that because they had never actually caught me stealing, they shouldn't be saying to people that they thought I was stealing. And if they said it to people, I was perfectly within my rights to go and beat them up, even though I had actually been stealing. I still can't make sense of how my head used to justify that whole thought process.

One day I got a phone call from my dad to tell me that a company his mate worked for were looking for someone to run a pub in a seaside town near where we had lived for years, and that I had been recommended. I was amazed. Finally someone could see how talented I was in the bar trade and had put my name forward. I made a call to one of the area managers to arrange an interview, and a few days later I travelled out to one of their other pubs to sit down with them. I was doing it again. I turned up stone cold sober, armed with all the things I thought they wanted to hear. They asked me what my ideal pub would look like if I could have it any way I liked, so I described this world-class style of sports bar that was in the shape of a stadium, with tiered seating, and the centre floor area looking like the pitch. This was someone else's idea that I had stolen. I can't even remember who told me about it, but I had a habit of copying other people's ideas if I thought they were good.

They told me which pub they needed a manager for and suggested I take a look then get back to them on what I thought. So, a few days later I went there with one of the friends I'd grown up with. It seemed like an ok place, but because it was during the day, it was quiet and we didn't get a proper feel of what the place was really like. Thinking back now, it was the typical sort of pub I was used to – not fancy at all, and the décor was pretty rough, but not the worst I'd ever seen.

I convinced myself that I could do the job, which was probably another factor of the denial. I still didn't know I was an alcoholic; in my opinion, I was just someone who liked a drink. Bar work was all I had done for such a long time, and I really believed this was my shot at making it in the industry and running my own pub. I went back to the managers of the company and said I liked the pub, and if they wanted me for the role then I'd take on the challenge. It was a win-win in my eyes, because it solved the problem of finding a job and also somewhere to live, as there was a three-bedroom flat above the pub. The manager who was currently in the pub was about to be fired, so they called me to say I could have the job but I needed to get down there quickly.

I look back on that situation with total disbelief. How on earth did I manage to convince a company to give me the keys to a pub and call me the landlord and licensee? If you've been paying attention while reading, I'm sure you'll already have a good idea of what was about to happen. I didn't, though. I still really believed I was going to be amazing at it.

So far, I've talked about the progression of the illness. At the start of this period, I started off as what I think you could safely call a heavy drinker. I was partying a lot, but the consequences weren't too great. However, as time progressed, I'd gone on to mess up everything that was important to me, and alcohol consumed my life.

Finally I had worked the pieces of the chessboard round into a position where I was living and working in a pub 24 hours a day, seven days a week. This would not end well.

Chapter 6
The alcoholic pub manager

When I think about that time of my life now, I'm saying to myself, "What did you think was going to happen, you moron?" But at the time I was still completely unaware that I was an alcoholic, and I headed down there on the train with my bag of clothes, in a smart shirt and trousers, full of excitement about this next phase of my life. I was going to go and achieve what I'd always dreamed of – being a successful manager of my own pub. Well, not quite mine, but you get the idea.

It started off pretty weirdly, to be honest. I was told to wait in one of the company's other pubs – down the road from the one that would become mine – while the bosses broke the news to the current manager that he was being fired and had to leave straight away. Eventually, I got a phone call telling me to head down there to take over the reins, so I grabbed my bag and skipped happily along the road. Unfortunately, when I got there, my happiness was short-lived.

The old manager had dug his heels in and said he couldn't just move out straight away. He told them he needed a few days to organise moving all his belongings, so he was going to remain staying upstairs in the flat while I took over running the pub. The bosses set new alarm codes to prevent him coming down into the pub in the night, and once I locked up for the evening, I had to sleep in a room above the other pub I'd just come from.

The way the company got rid of this guy so quickly, and expected him to just leave with all his stuff that day, should have set alarm bells ringing for me, but I just thought this was my only shot at making something of my life and went along with it.

On the first day, I met the staff members and assured them they still had jobs there. But it was around that point that the area manager decided to inform me that the pub had a reputation for trouble and drugs, and they had got me in to try and clean the place up. Clearly, they must have seen me in a very different way to how I saw myself. In my mind I was a scared little boy who ran away from any confrontation, so how did they expect me to clean things up?

I quickly learned from chatting to a few locals that it was actually one of the roughest pubs in the town. And what made the situation even harder was that the deal I was on meant I got paid a percentage of the gross takings. So if I banned all the rough people, I wouldn't have anyone in there spending money. Basically, my choice was to earn no money for a while and try to gain a better reputation, or keep the pub full of the people who the company thought were giving it the bad name and make money.

What really happened was that many of the people who had previously been banned by the old landlord soon heard that the pub was under new management and began slowly creeping back. And because I had no idea who they were, I just allowed everyone in. It was a decision that would come back to bite me right in the ass very soon.

In the first few weeks, as I was finding my feet and getting to know a lot of the locals, I always set out with the intention not to drink any alcohol myself until at least 7pm. But I think I failed pretty much every day. Most mornings the town alcoholic would come in first thing, order a pint, and offer me one. And after about two seconds of trying to resist, I would say, "Oh go on then, one won't hurt." It's funny how I could label him as an alcoholic but not myself. And even then I still really thought that one pint wouldn't hurt.

Bear in mind that I hadn't earned any money yet, and I was still broke from being out of work for a while, so I couldn't pay for any drinks I had. The deal with the pub was that when you did your paperwork at the end of the day, you had to write in any drinks you had yourself, and this would be taken into account when the area manager did a stock take, with the cost price being taken off your wages. I don't think I ever made a proper list of the drinks I had; I couldn't put the true figure in or the company would know how much I was drinking. So, from day one I was helping myself to drinks that I didn't pay for, and as I didn't write them down either, the stock takes were going to be skewed straight away. Not the best start at all.

To make matters worse, one of my old friends from the city where I grew up had moved to the same seaside town a few years earlier, and he had a reputation locally for being quite a hard person. Realising I was in the roughest pub in town, and being petrified inside, I thought it would be a great idea to meet up with my old mate and make it public knowledge we were good friends – a bit like an insurance policy. It wasn't the only reason I met him, though; he was a good mate from my earlier bar working days back home. But I saw this as a win-win situation: I meet up with an old mate, and at the same time send a little warning to any would-be troublemakers. Unfortunately, meeting up with him meant going out drinking to other bars in town, and I had no money, so I took cash from the till with the intention that I would balance things up when I got paid. Again, I fully believed that would actually happen.

My mate was quite a big drinker, too, and on one of the occasions we met up, we and were out pretty much all day. I'd run out of money, so we went back to my bar to have more drink, knowing I didn't have to worry about paying there straight away. I'd got quite bloated from lager, so decided that Southern Comfort was the way forward, and by the end of the night I'd managed to finish off nearly a whole bottle. Oops.

The next morning I was wondering how I was going to fix the mess of being a whole bottle short, as there was no way I could declare in my paperwork that I'd had that much in one day. Quite early on, one of the locals came in, and I knew he was well known for being a shoplifter as he'd previously tried to sell me stolen goods. I asked him if it was possible for him to acquire a bottle of Southern Comfort which I could buy from him. He agreed, and about an hour later came back with the bottle, asking for £5 for it. I didn't have any money at the time, so I dipped into the till again.

I had a bright idea to fix the till being £5 short, though. When the local in question bought the two pints he was going to drink with that £5, I would just not ring them through the till, and the money would be sound again. The bottle of Southern Comfort was replaced; the till was right again; and I'd just be two pints of lager down. I was feeling like a genius, with all my problems solved. Two pints of lager could easily be accounted for as just spillage, the money for that day would be correct, and everyone would be a winner.

How I thought any of that was a good idea or would even achieve anything is still a mystery to me. But that is how the alcoholic head works. My stock was already massively down due to the amount I'd been drinking, and the cash was short due to the money I had borrowed out of my wages. And if the stock was down when they did a stock take, I wouldn't receive any commission. This whole messing around replacing the Southern Comfort was completely pointless, yet I thought I'd won some sort of game with my bosses. But whatever game I thought I was playing, I was losing badly.

One weekend night, the bar was pretty busy with a good atmosphere. One of the locals pointed out a guy that looked pretty rough, suggesting he would be worth keeping an eye on as he used to be banned. By that point the guy was already in and had been served, so it wasn't worth the trouble of try-ing to get him to leave straight away. I decided to let him stay without mentioning what I had just been told.

A bit later, the pub suddenly became much busier with people I hadn't seen before. Something didn't feel right at all, and I could sense something was brewing. The dodgy look-ing guy I'd been warned about was standing at the bar talking to someone, when suddenly another guy punched him from the side. As he hit the floor, about seven or eight other peo-ple joined in and were all punching and kicking this lad on the ground.

I ran around from behind the bar to try and help him. I'm not sure where I grew a set of bollocks from so quickly, but there I was, putting myself between him and the people try-ing to attack him. While I was creating space for him, I was pushing people away, and eventually he made it back to his feet. I'd never seen a bar fight like it in real life; it was the kind of scene you see in a movie. Glasses being smashed every-where, tables being knocked over, different groups of people fighting all over the pub. The guy who had been attacked moved up towards the pool table and started fighting a few people off, but somehow he ended up falling back against the window, which smashed straight through. After a while, everyone that had been fighting left, leaving me with a right mess and a smashed window. Glass from the broken window was scattered all over the pool table and outside in the seat-ing area, there were a few broken glasses on the floor from the fighting, and there was blood all over the place. Absolute carnage.

I heard later that the guy had a rivalry with someone from a neighbouring town, and when he had been spotted in my bar, someone had made a phone call, and the big group of people that arrived came because they knew he was there. This was where not knowing who was banned had come back to bite me in the ass. The locals were pretty switched on to what was happening, and when an outsider like me came in, they took full advantage of the fact you had very limited information.

This was the usual kind of vibe for a while. You never knew who had upset who, and the atmosphere just always seemed a bit on edge as though a fight could break out at any point. In those days, the place didn't need to have door staff as part of the licence, so I had to deal with that side of things on my own at weekends. I tried to get friendly with some of the locals to get a better idea of what was likely to happen, but I think most of them just used me for what they could get out of me. I tried not to show any weakness, but again it was like I had some sort of bullshit suit on pretending I knew how to handle myself.

The young lad I had working there was shocked that I was running the place. One day he was trying to figure me out and started pushing me around a little bit, saying, "Show me what you know. You must know something. There is no way they would put a 23-year-old in here to run this pub if he didn't know how to handle himself." He must have thought I was a master in some form of martial arts, but I only had a black belt in bullshitting and that wasn't going to save me when I was called upon to protect myself or the pub. I just laughed his comments off, saying I couldn't tell him what I knew. I think the mystery threw him off a bit and he didn't ask again.

I was called into action one night for real, though. Two guys were sitting at the bar chatting when, out of nowhere, one punched the other. The assailant was huge, but I was the only person there, so I ran from behind the bar to try and stop the fight. The massive guy lifted a stool above his head and tried to throw it at me, but I ducked, and it bounced off my arm that I'd lifted up to protect my head. Then I just launched myself at the bloke and managed to get my arm around his neck, dragging him to the floor. My years of watching MMA must have been where I learnt this technique without knowing I could do it.

I dragged him out of the door, onto the steps that led up to the street level, and told him to please leave quietly – but not in such a nice way. As he stumbled off down the road, my adrenaline was going insane, and my legs were shaking like never before. When I walked back in, the whole bar started cheering me for what I'd just done and saying they wouldn't want to mess with me. I knew it would help me to keep order if people thought I was fearless. So I played on that a bit and made out like I was some sort of hard man, but it didn't change how I felt inside. I guess what happened was my fight or flight response to the situation had kicked in, but when you're the manager of the bar, running away isn't really an option so I had to stay and fight.

What I didn't know was that the guy I'd just thrown out had been in another pub earlier in the evening, and on being asked to leave had punched and knocked out the landlord. Without knowing it, I was going up against someone who had already been punching pub managers earlier in the day. He was also well known in the area as being a bit of a nutcase, and there was a rumour that someone had owed him money once, and to sort out the issue he and his brother had thrown the said person off the bridge that connected the town to the village on the other side of the river. It sounds worse than it is, as it's not a really high bridge so a fall wouldn't be enough to kill someone, but it would definitely cause some pretty nasty injuries. As you can imagine, for weeks I was absolutely petrified that this man was going to come back for me because I'd thrown him out. Luckily, it never happened.

The whole time I was there, I found it hard to find a balance. Because I was being paid a percentage of the takings, I had to sell as much as possible. This meant that when the bar was full at closing time and the punters wanted to stay for more, it made sense for me to have a lock-in and keep serving them. But that also meant I was awake till the early hours of the morning, and obviously I was drinking with them as well. Then I'd need to get up early in the morning to let the cleaner in and start getting ready for the next day. So, I was living on not much sleep and a diet of the odd takeaway and way too much lager.

One evening, me and three other lads decided to go clubbing in a town nearby. And after the club kicked out, we went back to mine to carry on drinking. I was still going at about seven in the morning, and that was the last time I can remember seeing the time on the clock. The next thing I knew, I was wakened by banging on the window. I got up, expecting it to be the cleaner, but it was my area manager dropping off a new TV set. I still don't know why, but for some reason I was asleep on the pool table with the duvet from my bed. I'd gone up two flights of stairs to get to my bed, then come all the way back down again with my duvet to sleep on a solid pool table. Two of the three friends I had gone out with were asleep on chairs in the bar area, too. I dread to think what my area manager must have thought. I can't even remember what excuse I used to explain what had gone on, but he probably didn't believe whatever bullshit story I'd come out with.

I could probably write a whole book on its own about all the stories I have from my really unsuccessful attempt at running a pub. There was a video someone had taken once where I was asleep on a table in the bar at 2am, with a load of people still drinking. The lad who worked there stayed serving people while I slept, and they filmed the video to try and blackmail me that they would send it to my bosses. By that point, though, I had stopped caring really. I wanted out but couldn't see a way.

Eventually, after nearly three months, the area managers sat me down and said the situation wasn't working and they thought it would be best if I left. They said they would give me a week's notice while they found a replacement. For some reason, I still pleaded with them not to sack me, claiming I could sort things out and I'd be fine. But I'm pretty sure they told me that one day I would thank them for making the decision, and that it was for the best.

And they were right. I was a shell of the man I had been when I'd left my home town to move down there. I accept I hadn't achieved anything up to that point anyway, but I had never really thought it could get much worse – how wrong I was. Three months of drinking heavily every day, not really sleeping much, and not looking after myself health-wise, had taken their toll. When I got home, my mum said I looked like I was dying. I'd lost so much weight and just looked a mess, but I couldn't see it myself until family pointed it out to me.

That spell running the pub was probably the worst, most intense three-month period of my life, and I made a real mess of it. I upset a lot of people, and I'm still a little bit on edge when I go back to that town, because I worry that I could be in trouble if I bump into certain people.

Despite so much happening in a short space of time, I still couldn't see that my drinking and the little bit of drug use while I was there had caused it all. I still looked for other people to blame for my downfall. And I still couldn't work out that I was an alcoholic.

The denial of this illness is what kills a lot of people. But how can we cause so much damage through drinking and not realise what the problem is? I had come close to killing myself health-wise while trying to run a pub, but it still wasn't enough of a consequence to make me take a hard look at my life or contemplate any kind of change.

Chapter 7

No consequence is big enough

By that stage you would think someone with the tiniest bit of intelligence would have been able to see everything happening in their life was due to really awful behaviour, and would link it back to the fact that drink and drugs were at the root of every disaster. I was always quite a clever person, but when it came to drink and drugs, I was an absolute idiot. I still looked for someone or something else to blame for everything that had gone wrong in my life, and I couldn't see that I was an alcoholic. No matter how major the consequences, nothing was never enough to make me stop and take a look at where I was failing.

At the age of 23, I'd messed up anything good in my life. I was kicked out of college after around four weeks. I'd had an electrician apprenticeship but got fired before my first year of college was finished. I'd messed up my first serious relationship. I was a father to a child I barely saw – and even when I did, my mind was on alcohol. Then I'd finally managed to convince someone to let me have a go at running my own pub, and you know how that ended.

When I returned to my home town, I was allowed back to live at my parents' house again. I think it was out of pity for me more than anything, but I still wasn't ready to learn from any mistakes. All I knew was how to work in pubs, so the first jobs I got when I arrived back were in bars again.

I actually lost count of the number of different bars or hotels I worked at over the next two years. Nothing had changed at all from the days before running my own pub, and I still needed more money than I could earn to fund the lifestyle I was living. So, I stole money from pretty much every place I worked, thinking I was really clever and that nobody could ever pin anything on me.

Thinking about it logically now, it was exactly the same situation as when I'd run the pub. I didn't have money to pay for the drink, so I just took it anyway; I didn't earn any money because the stock was always down, so every penny I spent wasn't mine either – it came out of the pub takings. The only difference when I was running the pub was that I had been stealing from myself, or the company. On the day I was leaving there, the final reckoning calculated the stock to be just over £3,500 short. That's an expensive three months.

Back home, working in bars or hotels, I was doing the same thing again. And when any manager suspected me of stealing, they would find a way of getting rid of me. I'm not sure why a reputation didn't follow me around the city, as most people in the pub trade knew each other, but as far as I know it was never a common rumour that I was a thief. The madness of this illness, though, is that whenever anyone tried to suggest I was on the take, I would lose my temper and go mad at them. In my head, because no-one had proved I'd stolen, they had no right to accuse me of it. As I'm writing this, I still have no idea where that logic comes from.

During that period of two years, I lost most jobs for either being suspected of stealing or for just being too drunk. To make my situation worse, I got kicked out by my parents again and was spending different periods of time renting a spare room in a friend's house or sleeping on someone's sofa.

After a while I started working in nightclubs instead of pubs, where I found the atmosphere more to my liking, but the same pattern continued. I just couldn't work there without a few drinks in me. It was as though I felt I had to get on the same wavelength as the customers. Yet I still didn't realise this kicked off a craving, so the whole night while I was working I'd be trying to sneak in more drinks that I didn't want to pay for.

Around that time, I began using a different drug that was slightly stronger than what I'd been using before. We called it billy or speed, but it is amphetamines to normal folk. And it was evil stuff. You could buy large quantities for a really cheap price, but if you sold smaller amounts for the usual price, you could end having quite a lot for free. And when you're doing that stuff every day, it gets messy. Several days in a row all merged into one, as I barely slept or ate. I was losing weight and just looked like a real street-level drug addict.

I had a constant need to earn money quickly. Once I'd run out of cash or amphetamines, I needed to earn a little bit to buy the next large amount. Then I'd sell most of it to try and make some profit, and keep a bit of the gear back to use myself. One of my mates, who was using with us, had found an employment agency where the method of getting work was to arrive at the office in the city centre as soon as they opened at around 5:30 in the morning. Then, as jobs were coming in, they were handed out on an almost first-come, first-served basis. The other great thing was they had a cash machine in the office, so at the end of your shift you would get the payslip signed by the employer, take it to the office, and then you could get your pay for the day, in cash, straight out of the machine.

I would go through regular up and down periods at this agency. If I'd earned a bit of money and got back on a drug session for a few days, I would turn up again after a few nights of not sleeping, sit there all morning, but not be given any work. I suppose it's not surprising really, as I must have looked a right state. The strange thing about this was that the whole time I was working for this agency, I somehow believed that I was the best person there, looking down on everybody else, thinking the managers would pick me for work before anyone else. How did I think I had the right to look down on anyone when I was pretty much in the gutter myself? If you sat there all morning till about 9am and no more work was coming in, you just left and came back the following day. That was a killer, sitting there with loads of people you really didn't want to talk to, for hours sometimes, on a come-down from drugs, and then just having to wander off again through the city centre, wondering what you were going to do with your day.

One particular morning sticks out in my mind. I'd been up all night on drugs, but I was running out of money, so I went to the agency to try and get a day's work. As I hadn't slept anyway, I thought I'd be first there to make certain of getting work. I didn't know many people up there that day, but got chatting to some guy in a big hi-vis coat, drinking the nasty, cheap coffee with powdered milk out of the plastic takeaway cups. It tasted like ass and burnt your hands, but it was still better than no coffee at that time of the morning. Me and this other guy had sat there all morning, and I was watching other people going out on jobs, but I didn't get asked. I was getting really wound up, but I didn't want to say anything to the guy behind the desk as I didn't want to risk not getting work the next day. When it got to about 8am, the guy I'd been talking to looked at me and said, "Looks like there isn't any work today. Do you fancy going to the pub?"

I didn't even need a second to process this. Before I'd even engaged my brain, my mouth had agreed to his request. We wandered off up the road towards the nearest pub and then realised it was way before opening time. So we decided to go to a shop and buy some cans instead, then wait for the pub to open. A little up the road was an off licence that was already open, so we went in there and picked up four cans each – enough to see us through till opening time. He suggested we go and sit in the park across the road to drink the cans, and I agreed that was a better idea than sitting in the city centre streets. At least we would be out of sight of most people making their way into town for whatever reason.

It wasn't a bad morning; the sun was out, and it was quite warm. As we sat there drinking, the guy was talking to me, but I wasn't really paying much attention to what he was talking about until I heard the words "It's ok sleeping in this park when the weather is like this."

I suddenly came round from my semi-conscious state, looked at him, and said, "What did you just say?"

This was a massive reality check, and one of the first times I'd ever honestly looked at my situation. It was 8.30 on a Tuesday morning, and I was sitting in a park drinking cans of Special Brew with a homeless guy. How the fuck did my life get as low as this? Then I realised I still had some cans, and I just thought, *Oh well, may as well just keep drinking.* So we drank the cans until the pub opened, then sat drinking in there until we both ran out of money then left and went our separate ways.

This was a progression of how much worse things were becoming in my life. Just two years before I'd been able to get employed in some pretty high-quality establishments – hotels, restaurants, golf clubs – and although I know I messed them all up, the point is that people were willing to give me a chance in some top places. I'd even been given the keys to my own pub. Now, though, I was being overlooked for work at one of the lowest end employment agencies in the city because I looked completely unemployable, and drinking cans in a park with one of the city's most undesirable residents. At that stage I probably looked like someone who should have had his own episode of *The Undateables*– the junkie edition.

Was there any fight in me to make changes at that point? If I'm honest, I don't remember making any big, life-changing decisions straight away. I do remember that a few days later I went to the guy at the agency and said to him on the quiet, "You know that guy I was with the other day? Me and him aren't friends." He gave me a look as if to say he was glad I had told him that, and sure enough I started getting some work again.

A group of four of us, I think, had been sent most days to work at one of the biggest removal companies in the city. The company was busy at the time and short-staffed, so they regularly needed a few agency guys to go on jobs. It was easy enough work if you were quite fit, and somehow I could still manage to put in a good day's graft.

The removal company had a big job coming up to move Coventry Hospital's entire contents from the old building to the newly-built site, and they wanted us four agency guys to go up there for about four weeks. We would stay up there Monday to Friday then come home every weekend. We were offered decent pay and overnight money, so we all jumped at the chance and agreed to go. Because I didn't want to mess this up, I stopped taking amphetamines, and we only drank a little bit most nights while we were up there.

After the first week, we all came back home and got paid the first lot of money, and I went out partying hard the whole weekend. It had been quite some time since I'd had that amount of money, so I took full advantage of it. I woke up late on the Monday morning, and as I didn't get to the warehouse in time to be picked up for the trip back to Coventry, they left without me. I was so pissed off with myself, and I ended up paying nearly £100 to get public transport up to Coventry to meet them on site. It was worth paying the money to not lose three weeks of work, though. Again, I had this really strange sort of God complex, where I expected to arrive to a fanfare and a standing ovation, with everyone being amazed at the great effort I had put in to get there. But the reality was that if I hadn't got pissed all weekend, I would have been there on time.

Somehow, I managed to hold things together pretty well for the last three weeks of the job. I never went out and got too drunk while we were working, and I didn't take any drugs at all. Doing that job on a come-down or with a hangover would have been too much, so I avoided it as much as I could.

It was quite a surreal time up there, as I was born in Coventry at the old hospital where we were moving everything from. There was a big building called M Block, which used to be the maternity wards, and I walked round it thinking I had probably been born in one of these rooms. I felt like it was some sort of sign from a god that I didn't believe in that I was being brought back to where it had all begun, as some sort of reset, and this was the moment I was going to turn my life around. But in truth, it was just little old me working in an old building where women used to give birth. Nothing biblical about it whatsoever.

When we finished that job, a couple of my mates who worked for the removal company said I should ask for a full-time job there. I spoke to the manager, and he took me through a formal interview process. I think because we had done a pretty good job in Coventry, he was happy to take two of us on, so I had a regular full-time job again. It wasn't the greatest pay in the world, but it was something I felt I was pretty good at. I had big plans in my head of getting a driving licence and seeing if one day I could progress with the company and get my HGV licence.

On my first week of working there, they sent me up to their depot in Oxford to do a training course. The travel and hotel were paid for, as was the food. I was doing an import/export wrapping course, learning the correct techniques to get furniture ready to be packed in shipping containers. As a result, I'm now pretty damn good at wrapping presents at Christmas time!

To a lot of people, the course probably doesn't sound like a big deal, but at the time it made me feel pretty valued. Someone was investing time and money into teaching me a new skill so that I could do a new job better. Staying in a nice hotel, eating tasty food, was not something I had been used to. In fact, until then I don't think I'd ever stayed in a nice hotel since becoming an adult. And my guts had no idea what to do with the nice, home-cooked food I was eating.

My stomach must have wondered where all the microwave meals had gone.

I really felt like I was at the beginning of a new chapter in my life. However, I wasn't thinking about not drinking. There was a big drinking culture in the industry, and quite often moving a family to another part of the country meant staying overnight, so most of the lads would go to the local pubs and sink a few. Maybe I went a bit further than the others, but the main discussion when you got back to the depot on a Monday was always how good the nightlife had been in the place you'd stayed.

I was excited about starting a new career. With the new knowledge I'd gained from the training course, and the certificate I'd been awarded, I went on my merry way to work on the Monday morning, feeling like a new man. I couldn't go and fuck this one up, could I?

Chapter 8
Moving the goalposts

It never seemed to matter to me how low I went, or how great the consequences, somehow I always tried to justify my actions. Things that would one day have seemed unacceptable suddenly became acceptable to me, and I would just move the goalposts and pretend that everything was perfectly OK.

If you had asked me a few years before, when I was assistant manager of a popular bar, if I would one day be sitting in a park drinking cans of cheap, nasty lager with a homeless guy first thing in the morning, I would have laughed at you. But when it became a reality, I justified it as not being that bad, and carried on anyway.

When I speak to people about alcoholism and they ask how low you have to get, I always say you don't need to be homeless, drinking on park benches, to be classed as alcoholic. You don't have to drink every day to be seen as an alcoholic either. And you don't have to be drinking first thing in the morning to be alcoholic. I was pretty much right down there at those levels, but because I had changed ever so slightly and found a new job, it was easy for me to blame that period on the drugs I had been taking at the time. And although I took the drugs away when starting this new job, I was still drinking occasionally, believing that I could continue with it and I'd be ok.

This level of denial is helped by the fact that drinking alcohol is so socially acceptable. It is seen as such a normal thing to do that people don't notice so quickly that their friend, partner, or loved one might be an alcoholic. Compare that to somebody getting into the same level of mischief while taking drugs. You would immediately associate the trouble they were in with the fact they were taking drugs, because that is illegal, and society tells us that behaviour is wrong.

At that stage, I'd put one period of drug use behind me and started my new career in removals. I call it a career, but I don't think it's something anyone ever dreams of doing when they speak to the career advisors at school. Still, I was excited again. Someone believed in me, and things were looking up for me again. I still didn't have anywhere I could call my home – I was using different friends' spare rooms or sofas – but I was working again, which was better than before.

My ambition to improve my life any more than this was non-existent, though. I would work all day then ask to be dropped off near my local boozer in the city centre. I'd built up a close bond with the staff there, and people who I saw as friends all drank in the same pub. The problem was – as always – that once I started, I didn't want to stop, so I would more than likely be in the pub till closing time, then stumble home and fall straight to sleep, then get up to go back to work. Most days I would wake up in the same uniform I'd worn the day before and just go straight to work so that I wouldn't be late. My personal hygiene was at an all-time low, and it wasn't long before the company received complaints from some customers that I stank of beer while I was working.

Again, this was something that infuriated me. How dare someone accuse me of stinking of beer? But the reality was that they were completely right. I kept going like this for months, just working and drinking every single day. And moving from sofa to sofa. Going round and round in circles yet again... but these circles were always on a downward spiral. No matter how many times I seemed to be gaining a level of control, it was always followed by worse to come. And this was the start of the next rock bottom.

Around that time, the Child Maintenance Service (CSA) caught up with me. I hadn't been very reliable at paying maintenance to my son's mother, so she'd had no choice but to contact them. And by that point I'd managed to build up a large amount of arrears which I had to pay on top of the regular payments. The CSA can put in what is called an attachment to earnings order, which means they tell your employer how much you have to pay, and that amount is deducted straight from your salary before you get your wages.

This isn't me moaning about the CSA or how they arrange to take money from fathers. I do have opinions on some of their methods that I think are wrong and need looking at, but I'm sharing this just to outline the situation I was in. I'd helped to get myself into the financial mess I was in, so I'm not blaming anyone here. This is just so you can see why I might have made the decisions I did.

The CSA told my bosses that my protected earnings amount was £104 a week, which is what they decided I needed to live on. Anything over that – up to £78 – had to be paid to the CSA. That was the regular amount I had to pay my son's mother plus a regular amount to reduce the arrears. If I earned over £182, the money was added to my wages. At the time I was on minimum wage, so my earnings were never much more than the £182 a week anyway.

Unfortunately, I got into a bit of a bad habit because of this. With the attachment to earnings order, if I worked three days, I took home £104; and if I worked five days, I still took home £104. The only time I was ever paid more was if I did a lot of overtime, which wasn't on offer very often. So, this took away my motivation to even bother going to work. If I woke up hungover two days a week and called in sick, I could still take home the same amount of money as I would if I worked every day of the week. As a result, I started calling in sick quite a lot, and the bosses became even more fed up with my attitude to work. I was either off sick, or in work hungover and stinking.

While in my local pub one night, I met someone that could get me cocaine. I wasn't getting it for myself, but it was a popular drug at the time and a lot of people wanted it, so I was buying it for them and adding £5 onto the price every time. A lot of the reason I was doing it was because it made me feel popular again. I was the man that people were contacting to get what they needed, and I felt like someone special again. This extra cash quickly began funding my nights out. The more I bought from my dealer, the more profit I made, so I could afford to be out drinking every night again.

Eventually, my dealer grew tired of me calling him so many times in one night and suggested I get the drugs from his supplier. This led to me buying bigger amounts in one go, and making more profit again. Small amounts grew to bigger amounts, and it wasn't long before I had enough spare each time that I started taking it myself. Over a very short period of time, things escalated until they were well out of control. I had even less motivation to go to work because I was making more money selling drugs than I was earning money legitimately, and the CSA couldn't touch my drug money. I was looking at it in such a warped way, though, and I remember talking to people and describing it as a new business venture.

Before long, my bosses at the removal company called me in to discuss my situation at work and gave me a week to sort myself out or they would be getting rid of me. I wasn't bothered one bit, really. I was making enough from the dealing that I didn't want to work every day anyway. At the end of that week, my removal job came to an end, so I was out most days just selling drugs to fund my lifestyle again. And my own habit was getting worse. As I got busier and was picking up larger amounts, it meant I had more cocaine spare, so I was taking more of it myself.

The thing with cocaine is that it gives you this feeling of invincibility, like you can do anything you want and nobody can touch you. One night I went to meet someone in the street to sell him a couple of grams, but as he handed me the cash, some guy appeared from nowhere and flashed a badge saying he was the police. He said there had been a spate of drug dealing going on in the area and asked what we were doing. I made some excuses and said we were meeting to go to my house – or the house with the sofa I was sleeping on at the time. He asked us to empty our pockets, so I took out everything except the two bags of cocaine my mate was waiting to buy. The policeman patted me down but didn't feel the drugs in my pocket, so let us go. I walked away thinking I'd got one over on the police because he hadn't caught me. Yet I didn't stop to think what the outcome would have been if he had found the drugs. I had quite a bit hidden on my person, and if I'd been arrested and searched, it wouldn't have ended well.

Even with this close call, I just couldn't see any other way than to keep doing what I was doing. I felt like I was living a high life, like you see in the movies about the big drug king-pins. I quite often had a lot of cash on me, so I was being all flash and blowing money on anything I wanted. But at the end of every week, I just had enough to pay the dealers what I owed them and pick up another load of drugs to sell. I was part of a big group of people that all hung out and partied together. A few of us were selling drugs, but all of us were using them. It was such a messy period of my life, but I thrived on the adrenaline rush I was getting every day.

My best mate had a flat in the city centre with a spare room that he was letting me rent from him, and it was like party central. Most weeks I would give him drugs instead of money to cover my rent; this was ideal for me because it saved me money, but I couldn't see how far down the rabbit hole I was going. Mixing alcohol with cocaine every day plays havoc with your mental health. Cocaine is a stimulant and alcohol is a depressant, so the combination left me without a clue of how I felt on a daily basis. One night out of nowhere, though, things took a major turn for the worse.

I was getting low on drugs to sell and didn't have much cash. I worked out that even if I sold the last few grams I had, I still wouldn't have enough to pay my dealer what I owed. It was normal practice to get the drugs given to you in advance and then settle up your tab once you'd sold them all, but if you didn't clear what you owed, you were unlikely to be trusted with any more. I called him to ask if I could have more on tick and that I would pay what I owed after selling that lot, but he refused. He said I couldn't have any more until I settled my debt. With no way of getting the money, and unable to stop taking it myself, I didn't know how I was going to get myself out of the debt. And I feared there would be some sort of retaliation if I didn't pay.

My solution to the problem was to take the remainder of the drugs I had to make me feel great and then end my life before having to face the dealer to say I didn't have his money. That night, when my mate went to bed, I stayed up playing his Xbox while I finished off the last of the cocaine I had. Once it was all gone, I went into his cupboard and emptied every single pill he had onto a plate then broke them all up into manageable-sized chunks. While playing a Tiger Woods Golf game, I told myself that when I played a bad shot, I had to take a few tablets, and if I played a good shot, I didn't need to. It seems insane now writing this, because I was literally playing a game with my life.

I'm not sure how it was ever going to work out in my favour, though; it's not like I was going to sit there for years playing great shots and never take the pills. So I kept going, washing tablets down with the couple of cans of lager I had left, feeling a little bit lightheaded after a while, and thinking this was me on my way out. Eventually, I finished the plate of pills, went to my bedroom, and put my head down to drift off. I expected that I would fall asleep and just not wake up again.

Strangely, I felt a real sense of ease the whole time I was doing this. I really believed that I was such a let-down to everybody that the world would be a better place without me.

My family didn't need me, and I was certain my son would be better off without me. I wasn't even in his life enough for him to miss me. The darkness you have to be experiencing in order to think that the only way out is to kill yourself is a feeling that is impossible to explain. Truly believing that I was no good to anybody and that I wouldn't be missed at all was one of the lowest points of my life.

At no point before, during, or after the attempt on my life did I stop to think what the fuck I was doing. In my head, it was a done deal. I was fed up of living, and I didn't want to wake up.

When I hear people talk about suicide, they often say that people who do it are selfish and cowards, with remarks like, "Leaving kids behind, how could they?" What they have to understand is that when you are so low in your life that you think death is your only option, there is nothing that will make you see differently. I had hundreds of really good reasons to still be alive, but my brain had flipped all those around and made me think I'd be doing the world a favour by ending such a pointless life. This wasn't a cry for help, either. I genuinely hoped I wouldn't wake up… and that feeling is one that still haunts me to this day.

So there I was, passed out on my bedroom floor, thinking I wouldn't wake up. My best mate had got up to go to work early, so there was only me and his girlfriend in the flat. She was asleep in her room, when suddenly a fire alarm went off. There wasn't anyone else in the whole building at the time – the people in the top flat had gone away – so we still don't know to this day who set the alarm off. But I was lucky it went off, because it woke my mate's girlfriend, and that allowed her to find me and call an ambulance. I have no idea what happened after that point; I just remember waking up in hospital with tubes coming out of my arms and my mum sitting at my bedside.

I'd seen the same expression on my mum's face many times before, but I wasn't sure what it meant this time. Disappointment? Anger? Relief that I was alive? I still don't really know what she was thinking that day, but when I saw her, I felt a horrible sense of shame. My first thought was a fleeting sense of disappointment that my plan had failed. Then, while looking into my mother's eyes, I started to feel guilt and remorse for what I'd tried to do. How could I have put my family through that if I'd succeeded?

How had things got so bad that I wanted to end my life? I certainly didn't envisage any of this when I started my drinking career as a teenager. The suicide incident occurred in early 2008, so I was 26 years old when I tried to take my own life. But at that time, I just felt like there was no other option. I'd messed up and lost everything good that had ever come along in my life – jobs, people, relationships.

Yet the idea of maybe stopping drinking or using drugs hadn't crossed my mind. The insanity was that I saw suicide as the way out over abstinence. To be honest, abstinence was probably a word I didn't even know the meaning of at that stage of my life. I'd spent so many years doing the same thing and training my brain into thinking that it was all I could amount to. I thought I was winning at life and couldn't see that I was only going further and further down. Nobody had ever shown me an alternative way of living that seemed appealing to me. In fact, I had no idea that other options existed. If you'd told me then that there are people out there who never drink alcohol, I wouldn't have believed you. It wasn't something I'd ever seen in my lifetime.

I spent a week in hospital recovering from the overdose I'd taken – a chance to contemplate what was happening in my life, and work out where to go and what to do. I had lost all ambition at a young age, and never really achieved anything in life. I'd lost every job I ever started. I'd destroyed every relationship I ever had with a woman. I had a son that was nearly five years old, and I'd barely been in his life at all. All my family had pretty much washed their hands of me. My drink and drug use had taken me to a point where I wanted to die.

This had to be the rock bottom that started the change in me. Well, you would have thought so.... But not for my brain.

Chapter 9

They wanted me go to rehab, and I said...

"Yeah, that sounds like a good idea actually."

I was in hospital for about a week in all – the last few days because I didn't have anywhere to go rather than for any medical reasons. My parents did not want me coming back home again, after everything I'd put them through in previous years. And my best mate told me that I was not welcome back to his place after what I had done, which was totally understandable.

That week gave me some time to think about what I was going to do, but I was all out of ideas really. During the days in hospital, some people paid me a visit. My dealer was one, although I can't really remember why he came. He told me I needed to get out of there as quickly as I could, or they would try and section me. That worried me a bit, but I realise now that the mental health departments of the NHS are so overcrowded and underfunded that it wasn't likely to happen at all. I expect they get a lot of people in hospital after taking overdoses, and a lot of the time it's a cry for help.

Not me, though. I had genuinely not wanted to wake up. I had no idea what tablets I had taken, so I didn't know what effect they would have on my body. It could have been fatal, or it could have just caused me pain for a while. But I did not know or care that night. I had just taken everything I could get my hands on and thought the overdose would kill me while I slept.

Someone from the mental health team did come to speak to me, but because I was scared of being sectioned, I told them what I thought they wanted to hear. They recommended I go to some recovery organisations in the city once I had been discharged.

I still owed my dealer money, which was my great reason for trying to end my life. So I had to work out that little problem, and to find somewhere to stay in order to discharge myself from the ward.

When one of my regular customers came to see me, my clever addict brain quickly came up with a master plan of how I was going to solve everything. I would sell him a large amount of cocaine that was roughly what I owed the dealer, but get him to pay in advance. Then I was going to pay the dealer what I owed him, get a load more on tick, and give my customer his amount out of what I picked up. I'd be in debt again, but as long as I didn't use any of the cocaine myself and sold all of what was left, I would be square with my dealer and back in business. Why hadn't I thought of that plan before? Not like it was a genius plan by any means, but it was a better one than killing myself.

I ended up staying with a female friend who had let me stay at her house once before. She was also a customer, so it was a mutually beneficial agreement. As a result, I quickly went back to old ways, as though my little trip to hospital had never happened.

Around that time things started to get really scary. I picked up quite a large amount of coke from my dealer, then for some reason he asked for some of it back. So I dropped some to him and he reduced my debt accordingly. I think he was getting himself into trouble with owing money and playing a big juggling act between people to balance his books.

A few days later, I was at my friend's house when my dealer unexpectedly turned up at the door. I went to answer it, thinking he might be coming to drop off the extra gear he had taken back, and when I opened the door he appeared to be on his own. He asked if it was ok to come in, so I said it was. Then all of a sudden, three big, scary looking guys appeared from behind walls and cars, and they piled in, pushing me back into the house.

My friend was at home with her kids, so she panicked and pushed the sofa across to barricade the door to the living room, while I directed the group into the kitchen. They started telling me I owed £2,700 to this guy and demanded for the money. I tried to explain that I only owed £700 because of the amount he had taken back, but he told them it had been returned to me. He claimed his mate had brought it back to me a few days before. When I tried to argue this and say that never happened, they told my dealer to phone his mate, and of course the guy on the phone backed up the story that the drugs had been returned to me.

Now, I have no idea if my dealer and his mate were both lying to just try and account for where some of the money had gone, or if his mate had been given the drugs to deliver to me and had taken them for himself. Either way, I hadn't been given them, but the big bosses didn't believe me.

Thinking back now, what was happening was the big bosses had come down on my dealer because he owed a lot of money, and they were taking him round the city to collect debts from everyone that owed him. To cover his shortfall, he must have been inflating everyone else's debts to save his own ass. I'm not even angry about this now, because it is exactly what I would have done if I had been in his situation.

However, it left me in a tight spot. I had three massive dudes from up north believing I owed a lot more than I did, and asking where it was. I didn't have it, so I didn't know what was going to happen next. I told them they would need to give me time to get the money together, but I was really just stalling.

The biggest guy there asked how long I would need, and off the top of my head I replied, "A couple of weeks." I knew full well that I'd still not to be able to get £2,700 together. If my dealer couldn't get any more for me to sell, how could I get any cash together – and especially that much within two weeks. It was another of those moments when my mouth opened before I'd thought things through properly.

The smallest of the three guys was standing propped against the kitchen sink, not really saying a word, which seemed quite menacing at the time. At this point, he stepped forward towards me, opened up his jacket slightly to show me the handle of a gun, and said, "You've got one week!"

The guy could have been showing me a water pistol for all I knew. I was certainly no expert on guns and had no idea what a real handle looked like. But I definitely wasn't about to challenge him and ask him to prove if it was real or not. I sheepishly agreed to his demand of £2,700 in a week's time, and then all four of them left. When the door closed behind them, I just sank to my knees and slumped on the kitchen floor. How the fuck had I got myself into this mess?

It wasn't long since I'd tried to take my own life because of a much smaller problem than the one I found myself in now. Yet suicide didn't come into my head this time. Let's be honest, it didn't need to. I was completely convinced that if I didn't come up with the money for them in a week, they were going to kill me anyway.

Understandably, the girl I was staying with wanted me to move out, as she was worried about protecting herself and her kids. I never told her exactly what had happened in the kitchen, but it didn't matter. The fact that three big, scary men had forced their way into her home while her kids were there, because of me, was enough to convince her that I needed to go.

The rest of that day was spent trying to find somewhere else to stay, as well as to come up with a plan of how I was going to get the money together. I had a mate who said I could rent a room at his house, so I went over there.

The crazy thing about that arrangement was that he was a friend who was also doing the same as me, but in larger quantities. And about a week before I moved in, the police had raided the place and arrested him with a large amount of drugs. The stupidity of some of the things I did back then still baffles me today. Of all the places to go and stay, I chose a house that was on the radar of the police, and continued to do what I was doing.

In fact, at a later date while I was staying there, the police knocked on the door and said they had a warrant to search my friend's premises because he'd been arrested again with a small amount of drugs on him. When they turned up, I was just about to weigh a load of the drugs I had and put them into separate bags ready to sell, so on my bed was a big tray with a large amount of cocaine. If I'd been caught with that, there would have been serious consequences for me. But because they only had a warrant to search other areas, and not my room, I let the police in and stood in the doorway to my bedroom, talking to the officers as though I was untouchable. They were in the house for around two hours, searching everywhere apart from my room and someone else's room. And I just casually left the drugs sitting on my bed while I wandered around the house watching them and talking to them. In the kitchen, I made a coffee while an officer emptying out frozen food commented on how disgusting the state of the freezer was. I was so close to being busted that day, and I was acting like I was invincible.

Moving in with him, I was still no closer to finding a way of finding the money for the big bosses and sorting the mess out. If anything, I was creeping slowly closer to either jail or death.

I called my sister and explained the situation, and she was horrified. She suggested I ask my parents for help, but I didn't want to go to them. I'd let them down so many times before, so I thought they would say no. But it was my last option really. I really thought these people were going to seriously hurt me or kill me if I didn't come up with the money. I remember standing in my mum and dad's kitchen explaining it all to them, and the look on their faces was horrible. As I was telling my parents the situation I found myself in, it sounded pretty unbelievable, even to me – and I knew it was really happening. Telling them I needed to borrow nearly £3,000 to pay off some dealers because I feared if I didn't pay up they might kill me, sounded like a scene from a movie. This was like nothing my parents had ever imagined would be happening in their world. But they agreed to help me.

While we were arranging to meet the guy to pay him, I dug my heels in and said I was only going to give him what I actually owed, and I wanted his bosses to be there to see I'd paid and so that he could verify the amount. His bosses saw this as confrontation, and one of them phoned me asking if I wanted to meet them with all of my mates and have a fight over it. However, when I explained that I just wanted them to know the real amount I owed, they agreed that was the sum I should pay him. While on the phone, he asked me if I wanted to work for them directly. I was shocked by this, but declined his offer. I told him I'd decided to get out. I didn't want that life any more.

We arranged to meet in the city centre, and it was the middle of the day and quite busy. I wanted it to be in a pretty public place so that there was less chance of things turning nasty. My dad had phoned a few of his mates who used to play football for the local pub team, and asked them to come and act as back-up. It was quite a strange couple of hours really. I walked out to meet the dealer with an envelope full of money, and some big, scary mate of my dad's grabbed him by the scruff of the neck and told him to take the cash and not come back looking for more.

Because I was in such a mess and was really adamant that I was going to make a real effort to change after this, my parents let me come home. I'd paid the guy off. I was living back home. I was relieved that the threat to my life had gone. This could be a new start.

But this new start, just like all the rest, was very short-lived. A few days later I found the boss guy's number in my phone's call history and called him to ask if the offer to work for him was still on the table. Within a week of getting myself out of the drug game, I had thrown myself headfirst back into it. This time, though, I was meeting bigger players to pick up the biggest amount I'd ever collected in one go, and getting myself in bigger debt. As always, it didn't matter how much of a mess I had been in before, I would completely forget, and my brain kept telling me that it would be ok this time. On top of that, I was struggling to quit using myself, so the easiest way for me to obtain more for myself was to get it on tick from a dealer and start back selling.

Long story short, I used most of this amount myself and was in debt with them again, so I started getting phone calls telling me to hurry up and get them their money. I was in fear of my life again, wondering how I was going to get out of the same situation. But this time, I owed more money for real, and to scarier people.

When I was growing up, a friend of our family had got himself into trouble with drugs at a young age. He had been murdered when he went to meet a dealer, and it was a story that totally shocked the city at the time. But even though I was aware of things like that happening to people I knew, it still didn't stop me from being stupid enough to go down exactly the same path.

During my stay in hospital, I had been seen by the psychiatric team and referred to the local drug and alcohol services, but there was a waiting list at the time. I'd be lying if I said I went back to dealing because of the waiting list, though. I went back to it because it was the only way I knew how to get myself out of the little bit of debt I was in. But by the time I got my first appointment with the drug and alcohol counselling centre, I was right back in, with even bigger dealers and bigger debts.

The whole situation was insane. I'd go there once a week and talk about how I was going to be getting off drugs and claiming to the counsellor that I hadn't taken anything all week. But the whole time I was there my phone was going mad, vibrating in my pocket with people calling me wanting to buy from me. I was sitting there with a few hundred pounds' worth of drugs stashed away while telling her how well I was doing.

I did, however, discuss with my key worker about treatment centres I could go to, but there wasn't any funding. I wanted out, and I wanted to get away from my problems at the same time. I'd heard about a centre about 25 miles away that was charity-run, so you didn't need funding, and my key worker and I started looking into it. We arranged a visit and an interview, so she drove me there one day to have a look, and I thought it might be just the right place for me to finally get myself off drink and drugs.

At the time I was always drinking in my same local pub and had a good friendship with the manager. I had always looked up to her. She seemed to be able to socialise and party with everybody, yet still manage to hold down good jobs and live a decent life. Well, that's how it appeared to me. When I mentioned to her about the rehab place I'd found, she seemed really enthusiastic and encouraged me to go. I hadn't been sure, but Anna helped me to make the decision, so I called them to arrange a date when I could move into the house. My head had decided that I was going to go there, get clean, and sort my life out, then come home and everyone would be proud of me, and I'd live happily ever after. That was my little bit of motivation anyway.

So, I packed my bag the day before and was all excited to get myself away from the city and see what I could achieve if I got myself clean and sober. I think it was the first time in my life I had actually had a clear intention to stop using and quit drinking, but the idea of not using any mind-altering substances scared the shit out of me. It wasn't something I'd ever thought was possible for me to do.

The house wasn't so much a rehab; I think it was more described as "a dry house". But I always just refer to it as a rehab because it's much easier when explaining it to people. I'd joke and start singing, "They wanted me go to rehab, and I said............. Yeah, that sounds like a good idea actually."

Chapter 10

Into recovery

While I was writing this book, my mother unexpectedly passed away. One day soon after, my dad found a small plastic wallet in her purse with a few keepsakes in there. He handed it to me and said, "You'll want to see what's in there."

I opened it up and there were photos of me and my sisters, one of my mum with all her brothers, and the first scan photo of her first grandchild – my eldest son. Then I found a folded piece of paper. As I opened it, I could tell it was my handwriting, so it must have been a letter I wrote that she kept. It said…

Mum and Dad

Just wanted to say thank you for all the help and support you have given me through the hard time I've been going through. Even though I don't deserve it because of all the shit I've given you over the years. You still stuck by me and that means so much to me. See you both soon, hopefully when I come back I'll be your son again, not the beast I've become.

All my love

Stewart

Love you both!

After reading this, I just stood in the kitchen and cried. I don't even remember writing this letter, but my mum had kept it with her for fifteen years, which shows me how proud she must have been that I found my way into recovery and started to change.

I must have written that letter to my parents then waited for the recovery worker to pick me up when I set off one Monday morning in May of 2008 to the treatment centre, with a spring in my step and just a bag of clothes. Full of excitement at the fact I was off to make a fresh start, I think I was more looking forward to having a roof over my head, a bed to sleep in, and getting away from the dealers that I owed money to. I would usually say that running away from problems isn't the solution because they tend to follow you, but this is what I was doing back then. I deliberately hadn't told anybody where I was going, and I changed my phone number to cut all contact with my old associates.

I had decided that I wasn't going to attempt to pay back the dealers; I was just going to ignore the issue and pretend it never happened. I suspected the drugs they had given me were full of crap, anyway, as there had been a speckled blue tint in amongst the big, compressed block of powder, which kind of looked a bit like washing powder. It did the job, but it was probably only about 10% pure by the time it got to me, so I thought I would ignore their demands for payment, and if I ever saw them again I'd just have to stand up for myself and tell them to kindly go forth and multiply.

The plan was that my dad would drop off the other few possessions that I had to the recovery centre. I've always been a big music fan, so a stereo and some CDs were all I had really managed to keep hold of over the years. I also had an old, rear projection TV that was cube-shaped – fatter than it was wide.

The process when you arrived at the centre was that you had to take a breath test for alcohol and a urine test for drugs, and if you weren't clean and sober you could not become a resident. I knew this already, as I had done some research on the good old internet and discovered that cocaine takes seven days to leave your system. I'd planned to stop using a week before my arrival date so that I'd be able to give a clean test. It had turned out to be a tough week, as I'd had no help at staying off and had basically gone cold turkey, as they say. I can remember going to a pub to see a few of my mates and forcing myself not to drink any alcohol while I was there, as preparation for the time at the treatment centre. I still don't really know why I put myself through that torture.

Anyway, I passed the breath test then I had to go and do the urine test. But to make sure you can't cheat, the staff had to watch you pee in the cup before they dipped the test kit into it. I needed to go quite badly but suffered from major stage fright because the guy was watching me. So, it took me ages to provide them with enough urine to do a test, and I was shocked when they came back and said there were traces of cocaine. I told them I had stopped taking it a week before, and we concluded that it would take me longer to show a clean test because of the amounts I had been taking. They agreed that if they saw the line fading over time, they would give me a pass, and I was allowed to move in that day. It actually took another three weeks before I was completely clean of cocaine.

The rehab was basically a massive old mansion in the middle of nowhere. The closest village had one pub, a phone box, and a tiny shop that looked like it was a few shelves put up in someone's living room. The pub staff were aware of where we were staying and knew not to serve alcohol to any of us. The idea was that you stayed in the big house full-time, and after three weeks you were allowed to go home at weekends but were alcohol and drug-tested on your return on a Sunday night.

During the week we did several activities to try and learn new skills, along with some education courses. They were designed more for younger people who were just starting down the wrong path and needed some help. There were people who had been sent there by their parents, or as a condition of an early release from prison.

The first few days, I felt a bit nervous. I suspected there were quite a lot of big egos in there, and I could sense a few trying to assert their male dominance in the group. My attitude was to keep my eyes and ears open, but my mouth shut. I'm not sure if I was seen as a threat to any of the other lads that were already there, but nobody ever made any attempt to start trouble with me, not even verbally. So I was left alone pretty much from day one – pretty similar to my early school days. I think because I was quite a big lad and looked mean, everyone assumed I was tough, and I just let people believe that and hoped I'd never have to prove it to anyone.

The first couple of months in there I was being a bit of a fraud. I'd left quite a large amount of the remaining cocaine I had with a mate and was getting her to sell bits for me, then collecting the money when I went home for the weekend. The way it worked in the centre, they helped you put in a claim for all the benefits you were entitled to and had it paid into their account. They took most of it towards the living costs and food, and gave you a small amount of the remainder to buy yourself treats and cigarettes, if you smoked. A few of the lads started to notice that I always had much more cash than I was supposed to and were asking what was going on. But soon the drugs ran out and so did the extra money.

After a while, I started engaging with all the activities that were being arranged for us during the week. I had gone there with the attitude that I wanted to get clean, sort my life out, and get back out into normal life, but I'm not sure many of the residents had the same ethos, and there were a couple of people who had been living there for years on and off. They would go through the work, get moved out to a flat somewhere, but after trying to live life on life's terms they would mess up again and want to come back to the treatment centre. Almost like a serial offender who becomes institutionalised and can't cope outside of prison.

Being in the centre was fairly easy; you didn't have to worry about paying your bills or doing your shopping and feeding yourself properly. The basic skills most people have were absent in most of the residents there.

There were different duties that were rotated every week, so we all had a go at cooking for everyone at lunch and dinner. There was also a computer room that we could use after we had finished our tasks for the day, but they had the slowest computers I've ever used, and with it being the middle of nowhere the internet was shocking. It was like having the old dial-up internet that hogged the whole phone line if you used it.

I'm pretty sure it was while I was there that I set up my first ever social media profile, and some of the earliest pictures on my account were taken at the treatment centre. Using social media, I was able to reconnect with a select few people from my home city – the ones who didn't ask where I was or what I was doing.

About six or seven weeks into my stay at the treatment centre, I found out the tragic news that my close friend Anna had passed away after being involved in a car crash. This was a really difficult time for me. Normally, when something bad happened, I would do what I've always referred to as hitting the fuck-it button, masking my pain with drink and drugs. Anyone passing away at the age of 21 is tragic, but this hit me harder. Anna was part of the reason I had found the courage to come to the centre to start my recovery journey, and now she was gone. I'd never get to see how proud she would have been if I succeeded.

After a few weeks of being down, I finally thought it would be better to use her death as a driving force for me to stay clean and to become a better person. I had used things as excuses to drink all the time, but never had I considered using a tragedy as a reason to do good. Anna's memory became a sort of higher power to help keep me determined to change for the better. So, I kept myself to myself and tried to work through all the education and courses they did for us so that

I could get into the move on group, ready to get back out into the real world.

It struck me as odd that a few of the residents – I would say over half – would go home at weekends then come back and brag about the fact they had been out on the piss on the Friday night and part of the Saturday. That way, they could give a negative breath test when they got back on the Sunday evening. It was like they were cheating the system somehow.

I admit I hadn't gone there with the intention of giving up alcohol for the rest of my life. I still thought that only the drugs were my problem and what I needed to deal with. But the rules of the house were not to drink or do drugs while resident there, so I stuck to that for the duration of my stay. Looking back, I think the drink and drugs had gone hand-in-hand for me just before I went there. If I had a drink on a night out, it almost certainly led to me starting sniffing coke as well. And I always knew early into my recovery from drugs that if I went out for just a couple of pints when I went home on the Friday night, I would be looking for someone to sell me coke pretty quickly. As I didn't want that to happen, I stayed off the booze as well.

One night, some people smuggled alcohol into the house and arranged to meet in someone's room. The next day it was clear that staff had been given the heads-up by someone and caught them in the room in the early hours. Now, although I didn't agree with what they were doing, I just kept myself out of it. I certainly wouldn't be a grass and get them all evicted. I learned, though, that people in the house were not to be trusted, and it made me even more guarded with everyone.

On one occasion, one of the other residents came back from a weekend at home and said he had bumped into some people that were looking for me. His story was that he had been on a train going somewhere and had mentioned the name of the place we were living. He claimed someone overheard him and asked if I was staying there, too – and said my full name. When he confirmed that I was, the group of lads apparently told him to tell me they knew where I was, and they were going to come and get me.

I was panicking so much, but he didn't know who they were and couldn't give me a description of any kind. So, I was left waiting for some people to arrive but not knowing who to expect. It turned out that nobody arrived, and I never did find out who was looking for me. In the end, I just kept my head down and got on with the work I was supposed to be doing.

I will say the place was a lifesaver. For me anyway. I got the impression that it's a great place to get help, but only if you actually want the help. A lot of the people were not there by choice, and I could see that they weren't ready to change yet. People only have any chance of change when they really want it to happen. But hopefully most of them at least had the seed planted so that change would be possible in the future.

I still see a few of the people who were there when I was, and a few have gone on to create a better life, but there are others who have gone on to be much worse than they were before. I recently went to the funeral of a young girl who was there at the same time as me. She moved out, got in with the wrong crowd, and was back on hard drugs quickly. Before long, she was found dead in an alleyway, overdosed on drugs. There was a lot of suspicion from her family that the people she had been mixed up with had murdered her and left her in the alley to make it look like an overdose, but I don't think a police investigation ever got to the truth. She was another young person taken too young from addiction. I'm starting to lose count of the number of old friends who have died from drink or drugs – either the substance itself, or from a suicide due to addiction.

I finally got into the move-on group, which was for people looking to get back into real society. The centre had someone who worked with the council to provide former residents with supported living, and they had a few flats coming up in my old home city. I was a bit worried about going back there, but I decided I'd been gone a few months and was no longer in the same circle of people, so I wouldn't have to worry about it. If I went back and kept myself to myself, I reckoned I should be able to stay clear of any of the trouble I used to be involved in.

They said they had a two-bedroom flat coming up for me and another resident to share together. I don't know why I agreed to this really, because he wasn't someone that I really got on with. But I think we just both wanted out of there so much that we agreed to move in together.

It wasn't a great position to be in, but it was certainly a million times better than before I had gone into the treatment centre. I now had a roof over my head that I could call my own. I was being responsible and paying bills – well, a little bit. I had to pay a bit extra from my benefit because the housing benefit didn't cover the full amount. And I wasn't taking drugs any more, nor had I gone back to the drink.

But the most important thing was that I had built up relationships with my family again, and they could all see how different I was now that I wasn't taking anything. I still had a long way to go, though. I didn't picture my life as being happy living in a shared council flat, living on benefits, and not really having any ambition, but it was a start on the right road.

It was a pretty weird time for me in the sense that everyone was happy that I didn't take drugs anymore. But nobody ever talked about me not drinking alcohol. I hadn't really thought about whether I was going to stay off drink, and it wasn't a conversation anyone else in the family ever touched on. I felt like it was expected that I would drink again, but nobody minded as long as I didn't go back to drugs. It's as though everyone thinks that because alcohol is legal, somehow it is safe to use.

The little bit of time I spent living in the flat was a bit odd. We were two grown men living together, not working, spending most of the day trying to find things to do to occupy our minds, and not really sharing any common interests. I could sense that he was getting a bit agitated, and I was concerned he would be drinking again soon. I had recently started dating someone, so I spent most of my time at her house, away from him.

Although I was clean and sober, I wasn't really in any proper form of recovery, so I think I was still looking for something to fix how I felt. And what better way to fix your feelings than by knowing that someone wants and loves you? I was seeking a relationship to fix how I felt, but I didn't realise this at the time because I was still in the madness of addiction. I thought I knew exactly what I was doing. But then, I always thought that.

Because I had borrowed quite a bit of money off my parents but only ended up using a bit of it to pay back the dealer, my mum and dad said I could use the rest to pay for a holiday with them and my son to Tenerife. So, in August 2008, we went on holiday with my boy, who was five at the time. It was great for me to spend some quality time with him after not really being around for the first five years.

But it was there that I finally came to realise that alcoholism and addiction is a disease that does not go away. And they continue to progress inside of you, even when you are not drinking or using.

Chapter 11
This beast keeps growing inside of us

This was a strange time for me. I had never consciously decided that I was not going to touch alcohol ever again, but I was enjoying a period of my life where things were looking better and I wasn't drinking. I just didn't feel the need to. Life was better, so I just stuck with it.

We flew out to Tenerife, and the holiday was going well, sunbathing by the pool with my boy, and going out on day trips. I remember we found a local supermarket that sold alcohol-free lager, and for some reason we all thought it would be a great idea to buy some for me to drink.

As the new Premier League season had started, my dad and I found a local bar where the football was showing. The first couple of times we went there, I somehow managed not to drink any alcohol – I think that was probably the first time I'd ever been out with my dad to watch football and it didn't end with me drinking.

However, the next time he and I went to the pub, I remember saying to him, "I'll be alright to just have one pint, won't I?" That same old phrase or thought that I would be perfectly fine to have one drink. So, my dad bought me a pint, and my intention was to just have that one while I watched the match.

Sure enough, though, one drink led to another, then another. I'd awoken the beast inside me again, and it was thirsty for more; thirsty for all it could get. We carried on drinking all through the game and for a couple of hours after, then we stumbled back to the hotel. But I still wasn't finished. We went to the bar, where they had a tribute act to Roy Chubby Brown, and we stayed there and carried on till kick-out time.

I didn't get overly drunk and cause any mayhem that night, but what struck me as odd was the fact that I hadn't had a drink for a few months, yet as soon as I started it was like I'd never stopped. I drank exactly like I had before I went into treatment. The next morning, I woke up with a really sore head, but we both passed it off to my mum that I had only had a few drinks.

I think during this period of my life it was easy to justify drinking to people because, like I said before, alcohol is so socially accepted that you can hide how bad it gets on the outside, and people don't see it as an issue the same way they would with drugs.

Back home from the holiday, I was in a new relationship and moved in with her pretty quickly. A combination of not wanting to live with the other lad from treatment, and using a relationship to fix me, meant that I thought moving in together would be a great idea. I then went through a period of a few months when I told her family that I didn't drink, then they would see me drinking, then I would say I didn't drink again.

That relationship went on to last for eight-and-a-half years, and we had two wonderful kids together, which was probably all the good that came out of it. It was only later that this relationship proved to be a driving force in me finding recovery from alcoholism.

During our first five years together, I returned to drinking again on a regular basis. From the outside looking in, it was probably my most controlled period of drinking that didn't result in as many bad events as in my younger days. But mentally, for me it was the worst period.

I had started a college course doing accountancy, because the teachers who came into the treatment centre had been surprised at how easily I had completed the Adult Numeracy Level 2 exam. I did my first year at college and passed the exams, then went back for my second year. I would always leave the house slightly earlier than I needed to, because there was a pub next door to the college, and I would go in before the lesson with the intention of having just one pint. That same stupid thought again: *Just one pint will be perfectly fine.* Sometimes I would succeed and have just one; other times I would be late for class because I had stayed for a second. It didn't matter either way, because once I'd had one pint, all I could think about was the next one. And during the whole lesson, I'd not be paying enough attention but just counting down the minutes until I could go back for another drink before catching the train home.

After a few weeks of the second year at college, I spoke to the tutor and was honest. I told him that I was unable to make it into college without going to the pub first, and that I needed to focus on recovery first, otherwise I would not be able to pass the exams. Then I dropped out of college for the third time in my life.

It was around this time that I made my first attempt at a 12-step recovery programme. My partner wanted me to go and get sober, so I tried it for her rather than for me. And I'm pretty certain it didn't work because I was doing it for someone else's benefit rather than my own.

I went along to meetings for about four months, listening to everything that was being said but not really connecting with any of it. Eventually I managed to convince my partner all the reasons why I thought I was different to the people who went there, and that I couldn't possibly be a true alcoholic.

This unfortunately started a relapse of a further three years and the worst mental illness I'd suffered. The reason it felt like the most controlled period of my drinking was because I spent the whole time wanting to drink the way I used to, but at the same time trying to drink in a controlled way so that my partner would see I wasn't an alcoholic. So, when I say it was controlled drinking, it wasn't me being in control; it was my situation forcing me to try and remain controlled. Anyone reading this who does the same will know exactly what I mean.

As a result, my drinking became more secretive, and I was very manipulative. I would ask to go to the pub to watch football, leaving as early as I could, start drinking as soon as possible, and drink as fast as I could in the three hours I could get away with being in the pub. Quite often, I couldn't even remember watching the match, because I wasn't overly bothered.

Concerned about my level of drinking, my partner would quite often try to monitor what I had, so I had to manipulate the situation, and it became a really bizarre game of cat and mouse between us. There would be perhaps eight cans in the fridge, and she would be able to see how many I had drank based on the amount left in there. So I would try and get a new one when she wasn't looking, but replace an empty spot in the fridge with another full can from a box of cans left on the floor near the fridge.

But then she would count how many were in that box, or how many empty cans I had on the kitchen side. At one point, I ended up hiding some cans under the stairs so that I could replace one in the fridge from a box she didn't know about. And I would throw empty cans up on top of the garage while I was out in the garden smoking, so that she couldn't count how many empties were there. Once a month, while she was out, I would have to climb on the roof and clear the empty cans I'd thrown up there.

I'll never know if she ever found my hidden cans under the stairs. But writing this now, I can only laugh about the ridiculous things I used to do to hide my drinking, and which I thought was perfectly normal behaviour at the time.

When she became pregnant with my youngest child, I remember her saying that if she couldn't drink during the pregnancy then it was only fair that I should stop as well. She even bet me £200 that I wouldn't make it to the birth without a drink. Really believing that I could do it, I accepted the bet as if it would be easy. Our neighbour heard this and decided to jump in and bet me another £50, so I stopped... for a while. I think I managed about five months without drinking, but it was another example of it never being my own choice to stop for any period of time. It was always because someone told me I had to or challenged me.

I had a trip to Liverpool planned with my dad and a couple of workmates, to watch the football, and I think I'd already decided beforehand that I would drink while we were up there then just deny it when I got home. That deadly combination of me, my dad, and football again – always a recipe for disaster. We arrived there at around 1pm on the Saturday, but the match wasn't until the following afternoon, so we literally started on the beer from the minute we checked into the hotel.

We had a few in the bar then headed into town. After going on a bit of a pub crawl, we decided it would be funny to take my dad to a strip club, so we asked around and found one nearby. I kept trying to get my dad to go and have a private lap dance, but he wasn't interested at all. Hats off to him for that; he didn't look like crumbling once. The funniest thing in the world happened, though. I came back from the bar and found Dad standing talking to one of the strippers. She had come over to talk him into having a dance, but my dad was still standing firm on his refusal. Instead, he began telling her that she shouldn't degrade herself so much by showing her body for money, and that with better life choices she could have a great career doing something other than stripping. I couldn't believe it! She probably made more money in one night than Dad made in a week. After that, we left and headed back to the hotel for a few more, and I think we only stopped drinking because it was closing time. And there it was again: I'd stopped for months, then the first time I began drinking again, I hit it as hard as if I'd never stopped. Most normal people going out after a few months off the beer would more than likely be drunk quicker. Not me, though. I carried on like a pro.

The next morning, we packed our stuff into the car, ready to go out for a bit before the game. Three of us went to the local Wetherspoons for breakfast, and I was so hungover I decided to have a pint straight away to sort me out. My dad said he didn't feel well and wanted to go back to the car for some more sleep. He is quite a big drinker and I've never seen him that drunk or that hungover, but I think I'd finally broken him. He looked a mess. What was supposed to be a great weekend watching my beloved Liverpool Football Club had become all about drinking again. And I don't even remember what game we went to watch or what the final score was.

Unfortunately, that was how it turned out with most things I did. I used them as excuses to drink, then couldn't even remember the event I'd claimed to care about so much. Drinking was always much more important than anything I was doing.

On returning from Liverpool, I couldn't even lie about the fact I'd been drinking, probably for two reasons. One: I'm a rubbish liar. And two: I didn't want to carry on avoiding alcohol until the baby was born.

I don't think my partner was surprised at all. If anything, she was probably shocked I had lasted as long as I did. And I never did pay her or the neighbour the money I'd bet them.

As we knew we were having a daughter, which was a first for both of us, we were both really excited. By the time she was overdue by nearly two weeks, my partner was trying all the usual tricks to induce the labour. One Sunday morning, I woke with the thought that the Liverpool v Manchester United match would be on TV later – the most anticipated fixture of the season. My partner said she was going out for a drive with her dad to go over some speed bumps – one of those magic tricks to make labour start.

Before she left, she warned me that if I started drinking that day and she went into labour, I wouldn't be allowed to come to the birth. Now, I don't know if I didn't believe her, or didn't care, or just hoped our little lady would hold on till the next day. But I'd already woken up thinking it was a match day, and I could justify a few cans when the footy was on, so the obsession to drink was already upon me.

I started drinking about an hour before the game kicked off and was three or four cans in just before half time. Suddenly I got a text saying she had started having contractions and I needed to get the hospital bag by the door ready, as they were on the way back to pick me up on their way to the hospital. My first thought was that I'd better have another can quickly before they got back.

Her dad pulled up and I got into the car so he could drive us to the hospital. But all the way there, all I could think was that it hopefully wouldn't be a long labour like the last one, then I could get out afterwards to wet the baby's head.

My daughter was born quickly, and then my thoughts changed to whether or not her mother would spend the night in hospital or come home straight away. I was relieved when she decided to stay overnight, as that meant I didn't have anyone to stop me drinking.

The next thought was what time I could comfortably leave the hospital. Her dad said he was leaving earlier than the permitted visiting time, and asked if I wanted a lift with him or if I'd prefer to stay and get a bus later. My partner agreed it made sense for me to get a lift, so it felt like the stars were aligning for me to get back home quicker and back on the beer. I knew I didn't have many cans left in the house, so I asked her dad to drop me near the shop, and I walked back home after picking up another 12-pack.

That evening, I sat there drinking on my own, celebrating finally having a daughter, thinking I was the best dad in the world. But what's painful about this story is that I managed to completely destroy with alcohol what should have been one of the happiest days of my life. Due to the initial obsession to drink, and then the craving once I started, I cannot remember any important details about the day my baby girl was born.

I don't know what the room looked like. I have no idea what time she was born, unless I look at a tattoo on my arm that has that little detail in it. I don't remember how long the birth took. I don't remember what she wore the first time we dressed her. All I can remember was being a slave to the alcohol, and it kills me now to think I was so obsessed with it.

My daughter probably doesn't know this story, but I guess one day she might read this book. I know she won't remember the day she was born, so it won't have affected her like it has me. But I give myself a hard time about it, because it really affects me and my mind. And it perfectly demonstrates the power of alcohol in an alcoholic's mind. Any normal person would have just made the decision in the morning to listen to the warning and not start drinking, then could have remembered the special day for what it was. Not me, though.

Unfortunately, this pattern of behaviour continued and got worse. Every night after work, I would be on my way to the train station to get home and think I had enough time to run in the pub, sink a pint, then get on the train. What I didn't realise was that as soon as I had one, I lost the ability to decide what would happen next. Sometimes I would still catch my train. Sometimes I would miss it and get the next one. Sometimes I would create an argument with my partner then stay out for hours.

I'm sure my partner must have been at home every day wondering which rodeo we would be on that evening when

I finished work. Yet I could never work out that if I didn't go and have that first pint, I wouldn't want to have more. You would think with even the tiniest bit of common sense I would have remembered how it had gone wrong previously and realised it was a bad idea. But the thought never crossed my mind; it was almost like the part of my brain for remembering negative reactions to drinking just didn't work at all.

At that point, alcohol fully consumed my life, physically and mentally. I was either drinking or thinking about drinking, wondering when would my next drink be, and how could I manipulate a situation to justify my need to have a drink. So even though my control level was possibly at the best it had been in terms of how much and how often I was drinking, mentally I was dying inside. And nobody knew it... not even me.

Chapter 12
My last rodeo

The 15th of May, 2013, started out like any other day, but it would end up being one of the most significant days of my life. The day I took my last alcoholic drink.

It was just a normal Wednesday at work, halfway through the week. I didn't wake up that day thinking I was going to get wasted later that night. But something in the day must have got me thinking about drinking. As an alcoholic, sometimes you don't even realise that you're thinking about it or trying to manipulate a situation where you can get to drink. The illness is so cunning that it works its magic without you even realising it.

I text my partner and said I was going to go and get a haircut after work. My usual barber had just been on holiday, so I was overdue for a trim. I called him up and arranged an appointment for after work. I knew the exact times the bus would get me to town, and roughly how long it took to walk down to his shop. He asked me what time I wanted the appointment, and without a second thought, my brain made my mouth say a time that was about 20 minutes after the time I would be able to arrive there.

So, without even thinking about it, I'd given myself a 20-minute window to have a pint in the pub across the road from his shop. My brain had just created that opportunity automatically!

After work, I headed into town, and sure enough was there with plenty of time spare, so I popped into the pub for a quick pint. I managed to stick to just the one, then walked across the road. My barber was still doing the client before me, and there was another guy waiting who was supposed to be after me. The barber apologised that he was running behind, but I said it was alright, I'd go across the road for another pint, and he could finish both of these guys before me. I made it sound like I was the doing the guy behind me a favour, but really it suited me to let him jump the queue.

What a shame he's running late, I thought, as I went and happily ordered another beer. While I was drinking pint number two or three – I can't remember how many I'd got through at this point – my partner texted to ask when I'd be home. I explained that the barber was running late because he was catching up with all the people who'd wanted a cut while he was away. But she knew the game and replied that I'd better not come home smelling of beer.

Oh shit, now I was in trouble! I tried to justify things by saying I was going to smell of beer because I'd had one pint while I waited. But I don't think she bought it. I wasn't a very good salesman when it came to lying about drinking. A text argument followed, and then I could see from my perch at the bar that my barber was now ready for me. This was the perfect scenario for me: I'd started drinking and an argument had started. At this point, if I went home straight away, I'd be in trouble, and if I stayed out longer, I'd still be in the doghouse. If the arguing continued, I could use it as an excuse to stay out and blame it on my other half.

As I was walking across to the barber's, I decided in my head that if she didn't reply to me by the time I'd finished having my hair cut, I would show her what she'd done by going back to the pub to carry on drinking. I can't remember exactly what message I'd sent to her, but I'm pretty sure it wasn't something that warranted a response. So again, I was creating an argument to justify my decision to go back to the pub and not go home.

After my haircut, she had not text me. But in all honesty, I don't think it would have mattered if she had. My mind was already set on drinking, and I'd set off the craving by having three or four pints already. I went back over to the pub and continued drinking, sitting on my own. I look back now and think it's crazy how I could be happy sitting alone, pouring poison into my body. After a while, the text argument continued, and I think it got to the point where either I was refusing to go home, or I was being told not to bother going home.

Some football came on the TV that I wasn't expecting, so I was pleased to sit and watch it. I think it was a European cup final, with Chelsea playing someone else. I wasn't really bothered, but it was another excuse not to go home. I've since checked, and it was actually the UEFA Europa League Cup final between Benfica and Chelsea. Chelsea won 2-1, but I wouldn't have known that without checking on the internet.

I remember feeling ok sitting watching the football, when suddenly the feeling came on that I was going to be sick. This happen quite often; I'd feel fine, and then all of a sudden that watery mouth and burning throat would suddenly come over me and I would rush to be sick. It's what I used to call the tactical chunder. Get it out and carry on drinking.

I rushed to the toilet, but I didn't run because I didn't want to make it obvious. Usually, if you are sick and the staff know, they won't serve you any more alcohol. More professional drinker tactics! I was violently sick in the toilet then returned to my perch as though nothing had happened, and carried on drinking.

My tipping point would always come at completely random times, and I'd go from fine to pissed in seconds. I think at that point I put a post onto Facebook, asking if anyone had a sofa I could sleep on for the night. It was a classic attention-seeking post, wanting people to feel sorry for me again.

One of my close friends called me to ask where I was, and said he was coming to meet me. I thought this meant he was coming for a drink, so I decided I would go to the cashpoint and withdraw all my money then take him to the strip club. When his car pulled up next to me by the side of the road and he told me to get in, I didn't argue. I thought he was going to find a parking place and then come with me. But he didn't. He started driving me home, which was about 15 miles away.

I asked him where we were going, and he told me I was being a twat and needed to go home, so he was taking me there. That was one of the worst journeys of my life. I knew deep down that it was all my own fault, but I was still always looking for someone to blame every time I made stupid decisions.

We pulled up at my house, and he helped me get in the door. After that, I have no memory at all of what was said between me and my partner. Everything was a blank until I woke up to go to work again.

That morning, I could sense from the atmosphere in the house that I'd probably done something quite horrible to upset my partner. We barely spoke at all, and she did not look one bit pleased with me. But that had become a normal situation. As the illness was progressing inside me, I was doing this sort of thing more often than ever before.

I went off to work with what felt like the worst hangover ever, feeling full of guilt and shame that I had no idea what I'd said to my partner the night before. I know I was never physically aggressive, but I could turn into a really nasty person when I'd had a drink and be verbally horrible to people, especially my partner. She was the mother of my children, and I could be extremely nasty to her when she objected to me going out for a drink.

Every time I tried to drink a cup of coffee that morning, I had to run to the toilet to be sick; I couldn't even keep water down. I could already sense that my partner had had enough, and even though my boss used to make jokes about it, I was starting to realise that if I carried on like this, I might lose another job.

When I was in the toilet, after being sick again, I stood at the sink throwing water on my face. Suddenly, I began thinking that if I continued like this I was going to be single again. If that happened, I would drink even more, and that would mean losing my job. If that happened, it wouldn't be long before I was short of money, and I'd be heading right back to what I'd worked so hard to get away from five years before. I stared at myself in the mirror and I just looked horrific. I was disgusted at the excuse of a man who was looking back at me, and I just said out loud, "I can't do this any more."

It wasn't quite the same rock bottom as trying to kill myself and ending up in hospital. In comparison, this rock bottom sounds and feels quite pathetic, but it is the one I remember as being most significant. It wasn't the first time I'd looked in a mirror and sworn I'd never drink again, though; I've lost count of the number of times I did that.

I went back to my desk and onto good old social media to declare my mission of becoming a better person. The actual post I wrote was:

"Been doing a lot of thinking today!! It's time to stop being a dick and sort my life out again. Meetings, here I come!! Thank you so much to (insert partner's name here) for putting up with me for so long!! Time to repay her for years of shit!!"

You'll see that I had another addiction at the time, which was the excessive use of exclamation marks in every post I wrote. However, the post did what I intended. I am pretty sure I was going to be told to leave when I got home from work that day, but my partner saw the post and changed her mind.

To this day, I still do not know why this time things were different. I've looked at myself hungover many times before and said I wouldn't drink again – and really meant it, too. But then I'd forget what a massive cock I'd been and start drinking again after a few days. If I'm honest, I didn't even know if this would actually be my last drink. I'd said I was quitting many times then started drinking again, so I genuinely don't know why I thought this time would be different. I think the reality is that I just wanted to fix the consequences I had created from the previous night out.

Not long before this, I had bought myself a DSLR camera and been trying to get into photography. But like most things in my life, I had found a way to make that hobby into a reason to be around alcohol. A friend of mine was putting drum and bass raves on in the city, and he asked me to take photos of the artists and the ravers at his events, to put up on social media afterwards. I'd been doing it for a few months, and it had proved to be a reason for me to be in a nightclub which I could justify to my partner by saying I was working. I really don't know how I could even see through the lens by the end of the night sometimes, as I was always so drunk by closing time.

I wasn't big into drum and bass, but I could just about tolerate it while I was working and getting the drink. Another friend of mine knew someone who put on hardcore raves and asked me to cover his events. This was much more up my street, and I was looking forward to getting started. The first one I was going to cover was a boat party on Friday, 17th May, 2013.

My last drink had been the Wednesday night of that week. The following day I'd declared my surrender to everyone and that I was going to get sober… and on the Friday I was going out all night to a hardcore rave on a boat then to a club for the after-party.

As it was a new event and a new promoter, I didn't want to let him down, so cancelling the gig wasn't an option. I was still excited to go, but I wasn't sure what would happen or if I would be able to resist the temptation to have a drink. The first recovery meeting in the town where we lived wasn't taking place until the Sunday night, so I hadn't even had the chance to get to one before the gig.

While I was at work on the Friday, the evening coming up was on my mind all that day. Before I left work to go home,

I had already justified in my head that it would be ok if I had a slip-up and couldn't quite manage to go the whole night without a drink. And it wouldn't be my fault because I hadn't had a chance to attend a 12-step meeting yet. So, before I even left to get there, I had prepared my excuses – a typical addict trait: pre-empt the failure and have a cover story ready.

This time, though, something changed. As I was about to leave to get a lift down to the boat, my partner said something like, "I believe in you. Go and have a good night."

I can't remember a time before that when anybody had ever said they believed in me. I was so used to being a failure and a let-down to most people in everything I did. Immediately, those words gave me a different perspective, and I began to think that maybe I could stay sober.

All that evening I was worried about someone offering me a drink and having to think about how to say no, as one of my fears was what other people would think if I said I didn't drink. In reality, nobody cares enough about me to wonder why I'm not drinking; they are usually more interested in themselves. And over the years I've discovered that if I don't drink, most people don't even notice.

The toilets on the boat party were below deck, and you had to go down some small stairs to get there. Outside of the toilet was a young couple snorting coke off a bank card. As I stood waiting to use the toilet, they turned and asked if I wanted a line of cocaine. I obviously turned it down, but I just found it ironic that I had been so worried about being offered a drink, yet during the whole night the only thing I was offered was drugs.

We left the boat when it pulled back into the dock, then we headed off to the nightclub for the after-party and I spent the whole night just drinking energy drinks. That was probably not much worse than alcohol from a health perspective, but for me it was better than drinking beer.

I couldn't believe it. I'd actually managed to attend a rave all night, surrounded by people drinking and using drugs, and I'd got through it without touching anything. I knew I still had a long way to go, and it had only been my first test. But usually, if I had justified a drink in my head before an occasion, there was a 99.9% chance that I would end up drinking. So, to have had the justification already and my excuses loaded in the chamber ready to fire off when I got home drunk, but then make it through the whole night without drinking, was nothing short of a miracle.

And to this day, Wednesday, May 15, 2013, remains the last time I had an alcoholic drink. And although the boat event was the first of many big tests of my sobriety, I've managed to get through those, too.

I am often asked if I would ever go back to drinking normally now that I've recovered. But I've reached a point where I don't miss alcohol enough to try and see if I could drink like a normal drinker. My life is so much better without alcohol, so I don't see the point of trying to add it back into my life.

I've had my last rodeo.

Chapter 13

Resentment hurts me the most

This statement "Resentment hurts me the most" can be read and understood in very different ways. Most people would initially read that it means, out of all the things in the world that can hurt me, resentment hurts me the most. And that is how I used to read it, too, until I met a wise man in recovery who explained a different view.

If I feel wronged by a person, place, or thing, and I sit with it for too long, in time that resentment hurts me the most. It doesn't hurt the other person, place, or thing.

This proved to be another of those lightbulb moments in recovery, when someone said something that was quite simple, but it was like a complete genius moment to me. I used to hear these people speak in meetings and wonder how they were so clever if they were the same as me. How did these people know so much about themselves when I was so clueless on how to live life?

When you first enter a 12-step recovery programme, the suggested method is to find someone you connect with and ask them to sponsor you. Essentially, they show you how to work through the 12 steps in the same way that they would have been shown by their sponsor. It's almost like family wisdom being passed down through the generations.

I remember asking my first sponsor when I would be taught all the answers to the tough questions, as though there is a sponsor textbook and an exam I had to pass in order to give advice in the future. He just laughed and said I would know the answers when the questions came. And he was right. I know a lot more about myself now, and sometimes I have good answers when someone asks me questions. But like everyone else, I'm still learning and growing every day.

Just as addiction never goes away, we have moments where we are in more control and it is always followed by worse relapse. Over any period, addiction or alcoholism is always getting worse, never better. And it's the same in recovery, just the opposite way round. Over the period of sobriety, we have many ups and downs, but during that period of time our lives will slowly but surely move in the right direction and improve.

There are plenty of tests in our recovery that we have to overcome to stay sober, and the biggest killer is resentment. But until I heard that statement from a fellow in recovery, I hadn't fully appreciated how much power a resentment had over our behaviour. A lot of people in recovery will pick up a resentment towards someone or something and not know what to do about it. They keep hold of it for too long, and it grows into a much bigger deal. What I call the fuck-it button gets pushed on the back of this, and they find themselves drinking on it. I'm not saying that always happens, but the majority of times when a relapse happens, you can guarantee that a resentment is hiding in the reasons somewhere.

I came close to this in my early days of recovery. I had a sponsor who gave me a load of suggested things I should be doing every day to maintain my sobriety. One of them was phoning him at an agreed time to check in, but I very rarely bothered. As an alcoholic, I wanted maximum reward for minimal effort, and the thought of phoning and speaking to someone about how I was feeling every day seemed too much of a pain for me to want to keep doing it.

When he quickly started to realise it wasn't just that task I wasn't really doing, he basically told me that if I wanted a sponsor to do things my way, I'd have to go and find someone else, because he didn't know how to do it that way. My reaction to this was to decide that I didn't need him, and I didn't need meetings. I was learning to box, was training in the gym most nights of the week, and had already had one fight, so I was sure I could just use training and a new friend group to keep me sober. As a result, I stopped attending the meetings through resentment, and I just trained most nights instead. I spent about five months away from the meetings which had been working fine, all because this one person pissed me off by being truthful with me. And in this case, the truth hurt.

And although I didn't drink in that five-month period, my mental health took a drastic turn for the worse. I knew I couldn't go back to alcohol, but I couldn't live without it. I began thinking there was no point in living. So that was me sober and feeling suicidal again.

I had expected to be feeling better by being sober, but off the back of a resentment, I put myself in a position where I was feeling worse. And to compound matters, the person I had a resentment towards had actually been right. I hadn't been doing what he asked, so it was my own fault. Some would say it was the illness at work; a disease that wanted me dead, the first thing it did was try to get me on my own so it could go to work on me.

I think most people in the world can alter their behaviour because they hold onto a resentment, but the difference for an alcoholic like me is that the change in behaviour for us can become fatal. If the alcohol doesn't kill us, then we can do it ourselves. If I think back to my attempt on my life back while I was drinking and using cocaine, the fact that my dealer told me I had to settle my debt before getting any more drugs had pissed me off. So, my resentment towards him had probably been a factor in why I did what I did. I wouldn't have known that at the time, though. In fact, until I started doing recovery work, I held resentments towards people I didn't even realise.

One of the steps in the 12-step recovery programme is to take an inventory of yourself. The common method is to write down a list of all your resentments: people, places, things; all of it. Who or what you have a resentment towards. Why you have it. How it makes you feel. And finally, what part you played in it.

As you can imagine, it can become a pretty big list. Most people build up quite a lot of resentments over their lifetime, and I was no different. I spent weeks writing this out, remembering all the horrible things people had done to me over the years. It's no wonder I drank!

Once you have your list, the next step is to sit with your sponsor and talk through it, then let it all go. My sponsor arranged for us to go to a really spiritual place to work through the list, and we sat in a quiet room above the cafe at Buckfast Abbey. He had called them beforehand to arrange everything, and we had a chance to look around before our meeting. The monks who live there sometimes hold meditation retreats, and it really is quite a fantastic place to visit.

As we were sitting there and I was going through my list of resentments, we come to one in particular, and he asked if I could explain in more detail what had happened. This is the story I explained to him.

When I had just turned 18, I made one of the no-win, no-fee compensation claims against an old employer because I had had an accident at work. This was back when the whole no-win, no-fee thing was just taking off. Eventually, I was awarded £4,000 in compensation for this little accident, so had a lot of disposable money. My parents had kicked me out and I was staying at a friend's house just up the road. It was pretty horrid really. My friend's dad slept on the sofa, while four young males shared the two bedrooms. We spent most days just drinking or doing drugs, and lived in pretty rancid conditions.

I became a bit frivolous with the compensation money and partied pretty hard for a while, and within about four or five months I was broke again. I couldn't believe I'd managed to get through all that money in such a short space of time. I had been given a credit card with a £2,000 credit limit, and I was withdrawing cash from machines on that as well. As I'd reached the credit limit on the card, too, I'd managed to blow £6,000 in a few months.

Months later, when I was living somewhere else, I checked bank statements to see where all my money had gone. I found loads of transactions that I didn't recognise from mail order companies, which had been made during the time I had been living at my friend's house. So I came to the conclusion that he must have taken my bank card from my wallet while I was asleep, ordered goods, and had them delivered to his address.

We had done something similar to someone else while I lived there, when we'd found a brand-new bank card that hadn't been signed on the back yet. We came up with a plan that I would sign the card, go up to the local shop, buy some cigarettes, and get £50 cashback. I think that was the most cash you could get back then, so I did that twice and we split the money. I've made amends to the card owner since, so I'm ok with that now. But it meant I knew what this friend was capable of.

When I totalled up the amounts on my bank statements, there was around £600 in transactions that I didn't recognise. My sponsor asked me how it made me feel, and I went on a long rant about how betrayed I felt, and that these guys had all just used me for my money while I had a decent bank balance. I admit I hated that guy for what he did. I used to tell everyone what he had done and what I would do to him if I ever saw him again. And I held onto that resentment for 15 years, still feeling angry about it while talking to my sponsor.

Then he asked me what part I'd played in the situation. At that point, I just started laughing hysterically. It had literally just hit me that this whole situation never even happened. Are you confused at this point? So was my sponsor. Let me explain.

I now remember that back when this series of events took place, one day my mum was asking me what had happened to all of the compensation money I'd received for my injury. Luckily, nobody knew about the credit card, so they all thought I'd only blown the £4,000. I couldn't bear the thought of telling my family that I'd spent it all on a big four-month drink and drug session, so I quickly came up with the idea to blame some of it on this lad I lived with and claim that he had stolen from me. I think I targeted him because I felt annoyed that I'd spent a lot on him and his family. Or I should say, they helped me to liquidate a lot of the money and drank it with me. As I'd fallen out with him at that point, it didn't bother me to use him for that purpose. It then appeared as though I hadn't blown all of it; I made myself a victim so people could feel sorry for me.

The problem is that I managed to convince myself that this version of the story was true, and for 15 years I completely forgot that I had made it all up, which meant I'd carried around a resentment to someone that didn't even do what I'd accused them of. Not only had I believed the story myself, but everyone else who lived in the same area had believed me, too. People would ask me why I hated him so much, and I'd come out with the same story every time.

This shows how crazy the alcoholic brain can be. That I could make myself ill by holding onto a resentment for that long in the first place, but also a resentment that was a complete work of fiction anyway. If I think about it more logically, my hatred towards him was possibly a reflection of the guilt I felt over stealing from the other person when we took the cashback from his bank card. All of these actions and thoughts had somehow become intertwined, but all just made me more sick. And it took me 15 years, and sitting in a room with someone else discussing the event, to realise it hadn't actually happened.

A great saying I've heard is: *"Holding onto a resentment is like drinking poison and expecting the other person to die." – Author unknown*

And there is another great bit of wisdom from recovery which I know to be true now. If I wake up one morning and I'm thinking about something someone did to me a few days ago, or longer, I can almost guarantee that the other person isn't waking up every day feeling awful because of it. Even if I'm in the right and what they did was bad, hanging onto it doesn't hurt them. It hurts me the most.

Chapter 14
What's the point?

You may have noticed that the first and last chapter have the same title. There's a reason for that. This is a term I used to use very often, usually when I'd tried to change and then failed again. What's the point of being sober? What's the point of being nice to people? What's the point of trying to achieve anything?

Well, I'm using it in a different way now. What's the point of this book? I'm hoping that by now if you think and feel the same way I did, you are able to see some of the things that I couldn't while in active addiction. Or if you are a family member of someone who may be suffering with addiction or alcoholism, you may now have a better understanding of the illness.

I'm hoping you can understand the difference between people who use vices to fix how they feel, and people who are addicts or alcoholics. As I said previously, nearly every person on the planet will use something outside of themselves to fix how they feel, and that is completely normal. And as long as they can recognise that they are doing it, it can be managed without causing a problem.

If shopping is your vice, you may need to look at curbing it if you are spending money you can't afford to spend. It isn't a chemical form of addiction, but it can still be destructive – to yourself as well as to your family. Your behaviour could be putting a strain on a relationship with a spouse. So even though you might not have full-blown addiction or alcoholism, there are times when your behaviour needs to be looked at.

The fundamental difference when it comes to an addict or alcoholic is the way in which the brain changes once chemical substances are added as a vice to fix how we feel. Most of us tend to use drink as a starting point, because it is so socially acceptable. Nobody really pays a lot of attention to what you are doing when you are on the first drink, or only a few pints in. They only seem to judge when you've gone that step too far and are causing problems. But even then, the person watching might even justify your behaviour for you and say it's because you just had one too many.

The other reason is that alcohol is the most easily accessible form of mind-altering, make-me-feel-good liquid that we can get our hands on. Anywhere you go, in most countries of the world, alcohol is on tap or on a shelf, ready for you to buy.

For an alcoholic, that first drink sets off the craving that we want more and more. So even before we have time to even think about how the rest of the night might pan out, we are already pretty much doomed to failure. We drink as much as we can and as quickly as we can. After that, to make matters worse, there is no off switch. The constant reckless attitude of 'one more won't hurt' means we go past the point of no return, usually to blackout, and then what's said and done is beyond anyone's control.

The other difference is our inability to remember our past mishaps when it comes to drinking again. The idea pops into our head to go and have a drink, and any recollection of the damage we've caused previously is not thought about at all. And our constant attempts to drink like everybody else always end in failure.

Some people relate this to a nut allergy, and say that if you're allergic to nuts then you simply just don't eat nuts. The difference is that peanuts don't make you feel like cocaine does. If they did, I probably would have crushed a peanut into a powder and snorted that, too. Unfortunately, we enjoy the way drink and drugs make us feel initially, so we go back all the time, hoping that somehow this time will be different. Our mind makes us think that it will be ok this time – and we truly believe that. For me, it was like my brain was playing a trick on me that my body couldn't handle. And I fell for it every time.

The last few years of my drinking became tiring for me, physically, mentally, and emotionally. The constant battles within my own head. The lies to cover up what I was doing. The lies to cover up the first lies. The feeling every day of not knowing who I had upset, who I needed to apologise to. I felt like I couldn't live with alcohol, but I also couldn't live without it.

If you relate to this and find yourself doing the same, you can stop blaming yourself. When I was still drinking and using, I thought it was only me doing this, even though I tried to find people and places to blame other than myself. But the reason we do it is because it is an illness. Anyone who keeps behaving the same way with drink or drugs is obviously not thinking straight.

Nobody wakes up one day and says, "I think I'm going to become an alcoholic or drug addict now." Some circumstances that lead us to our first use might be our own fault, but the disease of addiction isn't. And it's about time more people starting to recognise it as an illness and treated us in the same way they do with other illnesses. Next time you encounter an addict for whatever reason, try and treat them with a bit of compassion and understanding rather than judgement and disgust.

The first step to a new life out of addiction to drink or drugs is becoming aware of it. Until you truly look inside yourself and admit that there is a problem, you'll never get anywhere. Awareness first, followed by acceptance.

I am certain I was born with this illness, and from as early as I can remember I was behaving with the traits of an addict. This doesn't mean that every child that acts a little bit like that is going to turn into an alcoholic; you only really know that once you start using alcohol, which will be much later in life. The other baffling thing about it is that you don't always drink like an alcoholic from day one, and it is an illness that could present itself in you later in life. There are lots of other illnesses that can be present in you from day one but can develop later in life, so why should alcoholism be any different? I've met people who have diagnosed themselves as alcoholic but say they didn't start drinking alcoholically until they were in their fifties. They seemed normal for years, but then something changed within them later in life, and they lost control.

And you should know that you're not alone. There are millions of people out there who also suffer from this illness that wants us dead, but who have recovered like I did. When I was drinking, I didn't know there was any other way to be. I had never seen an alternative that sounded appealing, and the idea of stopping altogether never crossed my mind.

I often say to people that while in active addiction or alcoholism, the constant denial you are in actually teaches your brain to think that what you are doing is the right thing. So, I spent over 20 years training my brain into acting and behaving in a way that most people would find disturbing and wrong. When you get into recovery, you need to start retraining yourself to live and behave in a completely new way – one that initially feels all wrong to the alcoholic's mind. It takes years of constantly doing things we don't want to do in order to try and make it the new normal.

I didn't want to be nice to people. I didn't want to do good things unless it got me recognition. People used to say to me, "Fake it to make it." If it's something you don't want to do, then you should probably just do it. We are not able to think our way into a new way of acting; we have to act our way into a new way of thinking.

When I first got into recovery from alcoholism, I actually wondered what I would do if I didn't drink. I was sure that life would become boring and I'd have no social life. In fact, it has turned out to be the opposite. Now that I don't drink, life has become more fun. I get out and do all the things I used to only think about. I have a better social life, and probably have more friends who are better for me as well. I thought I was living a great life while in addiction, but the truth is it was actually very limited. Most days were spent in a bar or someone's house, with no real friends, just like-minded people who wanted the same as me. Those kinds of people would drop you once their need for you ran out, so there were no real friendships. And I had no family in my life either.

Of all the things recovery has given me, family is the most important. I have a better life when it comes to all the everyday things like a job, a car, somewhere to live, and nice clothes. But those material things are not important; they come and go all the time. The most important thing I've gained is something money cannot buy. And that is real relationships with my family again. My parents were finally proud of me for turning my life around and being the son they wanted. I was at peace with the hurt I had caused my mother when she passed away, knowing that she was proud of me. My sisters have their brother back, and I can actually be present in the lives of my niece and nephews. I like to think I'm the cool uncle of the family, although I probably just annoy them. But I can live with that over not being part of their lives.

And I am a better role model to my own children. Being there mentally and emotionally, rather than just a physical shell that is empty. During the writing of this book, I took my 12-year-old son to his first game to watch Liverpool play at Anfield. The number of changes I needed to make in my life to make something like this even possible is ridiculous. Having to be sober, be present in his life, passing my driving test, owning a reliable car, having the financial freedom to pay for it all; the list is endless. But to see the look on his face when Bobby Firmino scored the first goal was priceless.

All of this comes with time; it's not an overnight fix. And I don't believe we are ever truly cured from addiction. As I've said before, the illness grows inside you, and if I started drinking again now it would be like I had never stopped. I have had to come to terms with the fact that I am just an addict, full stop. I can quite easily cause problems in my life without a drink or a drug.

What I mean is that it is natural for us to start using other vices to fix how we feel, because that's human nature and it isn't uncommon. But as an addict or alcoholic, we can quite easily take any of these vices to an extreme, unlike a normal person. I can find myself acting out in other areas of my life which I need to keep a close eye on. For example, I have a pretty unhealthy obsession with trainers. I have a ridiculous amount of trainers that are in new condition because I only wear them a few times then change to another pair. And sometimes I buy two or three pairs within a short space of time. At this present moment, I'm not causing myself any problems with that. But if I was spending my rent money on shoes, then I would have to look at the situation differently and limit myself to only buying some when I could afford it, and after all my bills were paid.

It could also impact on a relationship. If my partner doesn't agree with my spending habits, this could harm our relationship, so in that case, again it would need to be looked at.

We can use lots of vices to fix how we feel, and it's ok to be a bit obsessed with them as long as we are not hurting ourselves or other people. A common mistake people make is using sex to fix themselves. They have the conception that as long as they aren't drinking or using, then it's ok. But that is wrong. Sex always needs another person to be involved, so if you're using it as a fix-how-you-feel exercise, then it's quite possible either you or the other person will get hurt.

It can be quite tiring at times to always be thinking about what I'm doing, checking my motives for everything I do, or every social interaction I have. But it is vital that I do this to make sure I'm not hurting myself or other people. The reason I have to do it is because the start of a relapse is not the day you pick up a drink again; it is usually months before, when you've started slipping back into old behaviour. If I do something wrong that causes a consequence, my old way of not having to think about it was to pour a drink on it. Now that I'm not drinking, I don't know if I can handle how I would feel if I did something horrible. So, if I start behaving in old ways, it's usually a slippery slope back to old ways of thinking, which could quite easily lead to a drink to block out feelings.

Over my years of recovery, I have found other things to become obsessed about, and I believe these are a massive factor in helping me staying sober. I started boxing at the age of 32 and went on to have seven years of training and 12 semi-pro fights. My addiction means I'm an all-or-nothing person who can't start something if there isn't an end goal, so I was never going to just train in a boxing gym. I had to have actual fights.

Once I'd been boxing for a while, it started to become easier. When I first started, the nerves leading up to my first fight were insane, but the feeling I had when I won was a better high than any drink or drug I'd ever used. It was a natural high that lasted much longer, too. But after 12 fights, the nerves before a contest were not the same as they had been in the beginning. I needed a new challenge, so I started taking dance lessons. Again, I'm all or nothing, so I wasn't happy just learning to dance; I had to compete as well. I haven't won anything yet. I have a second and third place trophy from dancing, so I've got a way to go yet.

As long as we don't pick up a drink, there is no limit to what we can achieve. I always say you will not learn anything sitting in your comfort zone. You have to take some risks and push yourself outside of your usual boundaries. Once you do this, you'll be surprised at what you will achieve.

I hope that what I've written has helped you gain a better understanding of this illness and offered some hope that there is an alternative life to be lived if you work hard enough. I've always been open about the fact I am in recovery, as I think people need to know where I have come from in order to ask for help. I guess you can't get more open about it than writing a book about your life. But if this book helps one person find recovery and inspires them to change their life, then it is more than worth it.

While I was writing, I saw posts on social media from an old friend of mine who was going through a tough time with a relationship break-up. He was using alcohol to cope with the situation and posted quite often that he'd got drunk and upset people. One night while working, I thought perhaps I should reach out to him and ask if he was ok, to see if he wanted any help. The following day I discovered that he had gone out drinking and then taken his own life.

I'm not saying that if I'd called him, I would have saved him, and I'm not saying that alcohol was the only cause of his death. But what I do know is that there is no problem in this world that is made better by alcohol. If you're going through something that's getting you down, the last thing you want to be doing is pouring alcohol onto the problem. It's like throwing petrol onto a bonfire.

Maybe if I'd finished this book earlier and he'd read it, things would have been different. Maybe if I'd spoken to him, things would have been different. I'll never know.

If you've got this far and related to anything I've said, I hope my story has helped you to see that you're not alone and that change is possible. We don't need to keep going further and further down; we can decide at any point that we want a new life and start to change. When I first found my way into recovery, I didn't really believe that there was any other way to live. I had no ambition at all, and I just accepted that my life was destined to be the way it always had been. Then I saw that a different life was possible, and I started to have hope.

By sharing our experience, strength, and hope, we can all change together. If I can do it, then anyone can. I believe in you.

Acknowledgements

Thank you to my dad. Whenever I needed you for help and advice you were there without fail. I wouldn't be the man I am today without you.

Huge thanks to my two sisters Tracy and Sharon. When I was at my lowest you never stopped loving me. And you both always hoped that I would find the right path eventually and be your brother again.

Thank you to Dan McNeill who has been my mentor and spiritual guide through my years of recovery. Not sure how it would have gone without you in my corner to advise me.

Thanks to all the team at Amber Foundation in Chawleigh, Devon. This place and the people who worked there helped me to build the solid foundation of my recovery journey. A true life saver.

Huge thanks to Cassie of Welford Publishing. None of this would have been possible without your help and support from start to finish. You inspired me to make a start on the book and motivated me to continue during every wobble I had.

Thanks to Christine for the genius editing work you've done to help take my writing up to a much higher level.

About the author

Stewart, who lives in Devon, England, has been described as an inspiration using his life experience to help others while remaining honest and humble throughout. Stewart has also been described as soulful and sensitive by his work colleagues while carrying out the outreach work with NHS staff. Other work colleagues have described Stewart as a playful cheeky chap who loves cake, I guess the sweet tooth comes from the addictive personality. But he is ultimately a true gentleman who wears his heart on his sleeve.

When he's not looking for his next pair of trainers, Stewart can often be found at a dance class learning some new moves to take to the competition floor.

He is a very proud father to his 3 wonderful children, Owen, Charlie and Isabelle and uncle to his three nephews, Jack, Aaron and Oliver and his favourite niece Louisa.

Stewart's mission is to end the negative stigma associated with alcoholism and drug addiction within the general public. And also help as many people that he can, see that recovery is not only easily achievable, but also much more fun that active addiction.

Contact Stewart

Website: stewartleeauthor.co.uk
Email: stewart@stewartleeauthor.co.uk
Facebook Group: Me and My Addiction, by Stewart Lee
Instagram: @Stewart_Lee_Author
TikTok: @the_recovery_author

Ingram Content Group UK Ltd.
Milton Keynes UK
UKHW020608030523
421151UK00010B/367

9 781739 097073